STORAGE PERIOD IN YOUR FREEZER

Product	Months
Roasting chickens, capons, ducks, geese	4-6
Poultry, stuffed	3
Fryers and broilers	6-8
Game birds	6-8
Rabbits and other small game	6-8
Giblets	4-6
Fish, lean	3
Fish, fatty	1½
Fish, stuffed	1
Sea food	4-6
Butter, sweet	12
Butter, salted	6
Cheese, Cheddar	4-6
Cheese, cottage	3-4
Cream	4
Eggs	6-8
Ice cream	2

Your Home Freezer

Books by Ann Seranne

YOUR HOME FREEZER

THE COMPLETE BOOK OF HOME BAKING

THE ART OF EGG COOKERY

DELECTABLE DESSERTS

by Ann Seranne YOUR

HOME

FREEZER

1953

DOUBLEDAY & COMPANY, INC.

GARDEN CITY, NEW YORK

I should like to express my appreciation to the National Livestock and Meat Board of Chicago, to the United States Department of Agriculture, and to the following manufacturers of home freezers for photographs and background material that made this book possible:

Ben-Hur Manufacturing Company; Crosley Division, Avco Manufacturing Corporation; the Coolerator Company; Deepfreeze, Appliance Division, Motor Products Corporation; Frigidaire, Division of General Motors Corporation; Gibson Refrigerator Company; Hotpoint Company, a Division of General Electric Company; International Harvester Company; Norge, Division of Borg-Warner Corporation; Philco Corporation; Sears Roebuck and Company; Westinghouse Electric Corporation; Wilson Refrigeration, Incorporated.

Contents

Illustrations

13

Your Home Freezer

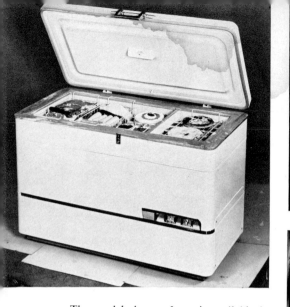

The model shown **above** is available in either 19.4 or 14 cubic foot capacities. The cabinet is divided into two sections. The smaller quick-freeze section is on the left. The larger storage section on the right contains removable baskets. **Upper right:** This 9.2 cubic foot freezer will store up to 322 pounds of frozen food. A larger model of similar design with 13.2 cubic feet of storage space will hold 462 pounds of food. The new counter-high flat top is an outstanding feature. **Center right:** A prominent feature of this 8 cubic foot freezer is its sloping front, which permits more space at the top. **Lower right:** Shelves recessed into the lid of the freezing compartment for extra storage space and interchangeable nesting baskets for greater convenience in the selection of food are new features in this model, which holds 508 pounds of assorted food in its 14.2 cubic foot interior.

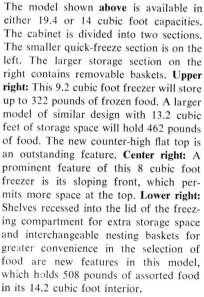

Special feature of this model is the 3.15 cubic foot fast-freeze compartment. The 16.35 cubic foot storage space, making 19.50 cubic feet in all, holds about 683 pounds of frozen foods. Three removable baskets make all foods easily accessible in the bottom compartment.

This model is available in either 16.89 or 22.53 cubic foot capacities which hold, respectively, 590 and 788 pounds of frozen foods. Special features are a "silent signal" that indicates that the temperature is being maintained, a container designed for precooked meals, and a handy basket for frequently used foods.

This model includes a 10° below zero fast-freezing compartment in either 14 or 19 cubic foot capacities. Stainless steel, counterbalanced lids, and a 4-inch-thick insulation are two of the special features.

Above left: This 11 cubic foot freezer is one foot narrower than former models. It will hold 385 pounds of frozen food, yet it takes up less space in the kitchen. **Above right:** A 20 cubic foot freezer that can store up to 700 pounds of food has a flat table-top lid for extra working surface, ice cube container, and four plastic utility shelves.

Below left: An 11 cubic foot upright freezer which has "jet-freeze" shelves for faster freezing, and shelves that adjust to five different levels for the efficient storage of various-sized packages. **Below right:** This 11.22 cubic foot upright freezer holds more than 390 pounds of food. Note the sliding basket which eliminates stooping over to remove foods from the lower section.

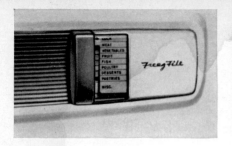

A built-in Freez-File for a planned inventory of stored frozen foods is a new feature in the 12 cubic foot freezer shown **below, left.** The Freez-File, on the outside of the door, determines what is in the freezer and where it is located before the door is opened. The selector is marked into 7 food classifications and plastic sheets record the daily inventory.

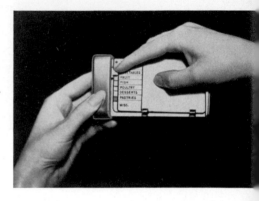

Below is shown a 27.76 cubic foot upright freezer with a capacity of 1000 pounds. You can freeze on any shelf. Other models are made with capacities from 18 to 55.32 cubic feet.

CHAPTER ONE

A better way of life

Your home freezer is modern man's latest contribution to the preservation of food. It is not simply a storage vault for bushels of fruit and vegetables, nor a place to hoard large quantities of meat. Rather, it is a miraculous appliance with unlimited possibilities; it can revolutionize your eating habits, give your family better meals, and allow you new freedom and leisure to enjoy other interests.

The purchase of your freezer is probably the biggest step you have taken to make your home more complete and efficient since you bought your first mechanical refrigerator.

How much pleasure and economical use you derive from your freezer depends upon you. It varies with each individual. To some the home freezer may mean larger storage space for commercially frozen foods. To those who live in the suburbs, or on a farm, it may mean an easier way to preserve the surplus from the garden, the liberty to slaughter at the most economical time of the year, or the elimination of frequent trips to the nearest food center. To others it may mean that meals can be planned well in advance, saving last-minute fuss or confusion, affording, too, the comforting knowledge that the utmost in hospitality may be shown to guests at any moment.

To everyone, the freezer should mean a new and better way of life.

Freezing food is the simplest method of food preservation, but it is by no means the least expensive. The cost of freezing one pound of food, when you consider equipment cost and depreciation, electricity, and the containers and wrapping materials for proper storage, is several times more than if you canned it.

On the other hand, there are no jars to sterilize and no standing over a hot stove for hours in summertime, for freezing is extraordinarily easy and consumes a minimum of time and labor. You don't save money, but you do save time and work. And foods properly wrapped and frozen are more nearly like fresh foods than if they were preserved by any other method.

Yes, everyone should have a home freezer to

1. Provide an almost endless variety of appetizing foods the year round.

2. Reduce, by the frugal freezing of leftovers, wastage of food.

3. Preserve vegetables, meats, fish, game, and dairy products that might, during times of abundance, otherwise go to waste.

4. Enhance the hospitality of the home.

5. Give the homemaker more free time for hobbies, social activities, and other household tasks, which more laborious means of food handling cause to be postponed.

6. Enable the homemaker to give and to enjoy, free of fatigue, many more special dinners and parties, much of the food for which may be taken from the freezer.

WHAT SIZE AND KIND OF A FREEZER TO BUY

The space that you have available may well be the determining factor in the size of the home freezer you decide to buy.

The homemaker who lives in the average American apartment with its limited kitchen space may be only too happy to have a 4-cubic-foot freezer to squeeze into the last remaining wall space in her kitchen. Naturally, she cannot hope to store in this freezer a season's supply of fruits and vegetables. She cannot buy a side of beef or a dozen ducks when she finds a bargain. She can, however, keep on hand a few packages of her favorite commercially frozen foods, a few steaks, some broilers, a couple of loaves of French bread, and many a ready-made dish to warm up at a moment's notice.

If space is no problem, the next important considerations in selecting a freezer are how you intend to use it and your family's mode of life. Unless you live on a farm or in a rural town, miles from a shopping center, a small freezer is adequate for most family needs. Before you make your final choice, however, you should consider:

1. The number of people in your family.
2. The extent of entertaining that you do.
3. Whether you have your own garden and wish to freeze the surplus crops.
4. Whether you are holding down a job and have the responsibility of both earning a living and taking care of home and family.

To help you make your decision, you should know that:

1 cubic foot of freezer space will accommodate 54 rectangular pint containers, 70 twelve-ounce packages of commercially frozen foods, or 12 frying chickens.
2 cubic feet will accommodate a loin or round of beef.
3 cubic feet will accommodate a quarter of beef.

There are three principal types of home freezers:

1. *The Chest-type Freezer* ranges in size from 2 to 22 cubic feet, with storage capacities of 70 to 780 pounds. It may be square or rectangular with a top opening. Most single-compartment chest freezers provide both freezing and storage in the same area. Those that have several compartments provide a separate area for freezing.

2. *The Upright Freezer* ranges in size from 6 to 55 cubic feet, with capacities from 210 to 2000 pounds of food. It requires no more floor space than a refrigerator and has a front-opening door. This type of freezer usually includes several zero storage compartments, and some provide a special quick-freezing compartment.

3. *The Walk-in Freezer* is really suitable only for farms or for commercial use where more than 20 cubic feet of space is required. It is seldom practical for average-family needs. Some walk-in freezers have a chilling compartment, about 32° F., for holding meat, or for rapidly cooling freshly slaughtered animals. Others include a storage area for root crops and winter fruits.

Points to consider when shopping for your home freezer:

1. All-steel construction will give longer service.

2. The steel cabinet should be given some rust-resistant treatment before the exterior finish is applied.

3. Plastic door gaskets are resistant to grease and last longer.

4. Baked-on enamel does not chip and is easy to keep clean.

5. Rounded corners in the interior of the freezer are easier to clean.

6. The opening should be well insulated, and it should swing up or out easily, on ball-bearing hinges. It should close tightly and have a cushion gasket surrounding the opening to prevent warm air from leaking into the freezer.

7. Inorganic insulation from 3 to 4 inches deep is vitally important to the maintenance of a constant temperature with a minimum of electric power. This is also important in the event that the power becomes interrupted. A well-insulated freezer will keep foods safely at zero temperature for as long as 36 hours with the electric current off.

8. A fast-freezing compartment is not necessary, but it is desirable.

9. Special features are the trademark of the different manufacturers, and it is up to you to decide which of these special features make one freezer more attractive to you than another. Some of these features are visible in the photographs at the beginning of this chapter.

WHERE TO PLACE YOUR FREEZER

Before you buy your home freezer you will, naturally, give some thought to where you are going to put it.

The first choice is the kitchen where you prepare the food to be frozen and later cook the frozen food. The temperature of the room does not affect the constant zero temperature within your freezer and certainly the kitchen is the logical place. Common sense would motivate you to select a spot away from the stove, radiator, or the direct rays of the sun.

The next best place would be the breakfast room, pantry, or porch, as close to the kitchen as possible.

Finally, the cellar or garage must be used if there is no room nearer the kitchen. Even so, a home freezer is worth these extra steps.

Check with your electrician to make sure that the electrical circuit for your freezer is not already overloaded. A level, solid floor is important.

If you are planning to remodel, or to build a new home, provide adequate space for a home freezer even if your present budget does not allow one. It may not be long before it will!

HOW TO CARE FOR YOUR HOME FREEZER

Having read this far, you have probably made your decision, and your home freezer is already installed or will soon be delivered. Specific directions for the care of your freezer are supplied by the company from whom you bought it. The following are general:

A home freezer is the simplest of all household appliances to operate. The best care you can give it is to leave it strictly alone most of the time. It automatically controls the zero temperature in the storage compartment and below-zero in the quick-freeze compartment. When food to be frozen is placed in the freezer, the automatic control provides the additional refrigeration necessary to freeze it quickly.

Defrosting. How often your freezer must be defrosted depends on the moisture content of the air inside the freezer, how many times the door is opened to withdraw or put in packages, and how moisture-vaporproof your packaging of the food has been. But once or twice a year should be sufficient.

When frost accumulates to a depth of about ¼ inch, it should be scraped off with a smooth-edged, hard plastic or wooden paddle. Sharp tools or wire brushes should not be used. Remove the food from your freezer and wrap it in several thicknesses of paper. If your freezer has a drain, the frost may be melted easily by putting saucepans filled with boiling water in the freezer and repeating after 15 minutes if the frost has not melted. Otherwise, scrape the frost onto layers of newspaper so that it can be lifted out easily. Work as quickly as possible and return the frozen food as soon as the frost has been removed.

Cleaning. Once a year your freezer should be thoroughly cleaned, and the logical time to do this is in the spring, when your supply of frozen food is at its minimum. It is also logical to clean your freezer at a time when it needs defrosting as well. Turn off the current and place all the packages from the freezer in a box thickly lined with newspapers and dry ice. Defrost the freezer and wash each compartment with a solution of 2 tablespoons of baking soda dissolved in each quart of warm water. Soap or caustic solutions must never be used. Dry the inside of the compartments thoroughly before turning on the power and return the food as soon as the interior reaches zero.

Does the motor need oiling? That depends entirely on the make of freezer you own. Many home freezers have the units hermetically sealed with a lifetime of lubrication.

What happens if the power fails? DON'T OPEN THE DOOR UNTIL THE POWER IS RESTORED, or if the power remains off for more than 48 hours, open the door just long enough to put dry ice into the compartments. It is a wise precaution to locate a source of supply of dry ice near your home in case of emergency. Usually your local dairy or ice plant can supply you. Handle the dry ice with gloves and pack about 10 pounds into each compartment. Fifty pounds of dry ice will hold the temperature in a 20-cubic-foot cabinet with a full load of frozen food for about 4 days. If the freezer is only partially filled with frozen food, the danger point will be reached in 2 to 3 days. A 6-cubic-foot freezer needs only 15 pounds of dry ice to protect food in an emergency.

Dry ice is not really ice at all, for it contains no water. It is the harmless, non-toxic carbon dioxide gas, first liquefied, then frozen to a temperature of 109° *below* zero. As it melts and absorbs heat, it evaporates to its natural gaseous state, leaving behind it no moisture.

Should an alarm be installed? Definitely! Sometimes the door to your freezer is accidentally left open. A temperature-operated alarm sounds a warning if, for any reason, the temperature in your freezer rises to the danger point. Many freezers on the market today are already equipped with this device. Be sure to have the alarm batteries checked occasionally.

OPERATION COST

How much will a freezer cost to operate? That depends on many things—the cubic foot capacity, the kind and thickness of insulation, the type of construction, the horsepower of the motor on the freezing unit, the quantity of foods frozen, the temperature of the food to be frozen, the length of time, how frequently the freezer is opened, and the temperature at which the cabinet is held for storage. But your freezer is going to cost you money, so be prepared for your next electric bill. Even the smallest, most economically operated home freezer will add at least $3 per month to your bill.

There are a few rules for the most efficient and economical operation of your freezer, and I list them here:

1. Keep your freezer in a dry place away from sunny windows, radiators, and stoves.

2. Avoid freezing too large a quantity of food at one time.

3. Keep the packages well organized in the most convenient place, so you can find them quickly and easily.

4. Defrost when necessary. Thick layers of frost inside your freezer reduce efficiency and make the maintenance of zero temperatures more difficult.

5. Chill all foods before putting them into your freezer. Warm foods raise the temperature inside the freezer and cause unnecessary use of electricity.

6. Two freezers are more economical than one. For instance, if

you decide you need 20 cubic feet of freezer space, two 10-cubic-foot freezers are more economical than one large one. The use of one may be discontinued during periods when your supply of frozen foods is at a minimum. Again, one may be reserved for those foods that you intend to store for a considerable period. The other may be kept exclusively for foods such as butter, coffee, cream, bread, rolls, et cetera, that are used every day.

EQUIPMENT

Except for a good supply of packaging materials, very little equipment other than that found in a moderately equipped kitchen is needed. You should have:

1. Sharp knives for slicing and preparing vegetables.
2. Measuring cups and spoons.
3. A large spoon or scoop.
4. A nest of bowls.
5. Two 6-quart cooking kettles with tight-fitting lids.
6. A square funnel, or a tin can with ends removed and sides flattened, for filling bags.
7. A carton holder for easier packaging and sealing.
8. A fine-meshed wire basket or cheesecloth for scalding vegetables.
9. A pitcher for syrup.
10. A thermostatically controlled hand iron, or a curling iron, for sealing packages.
11. A labeling pencil.

PACKAGING MATERIALS

Much of the success of home-frozen foods depends upon proper packaging materials and how foods are wrapped and sealed for storage, so the importance of this phase of freezing cannot be over-emphasized. There must be no exchange of moisture or air between the frozen food and the air inside the cabinet. Cold air is dry air and dry air will draw the moisture from the foods unless they are protected by moisture-vaporproof materials, which are readily available and which were designed expressly to exclude the air and prevent the escape of moisture from frozen foods.

The meaning of *moisture-vaporproof* should not be confused with the word waterproof. Ordinary wax or oil papers, gift-wrap Cellophanes, and ice-cream cartons, while waterproof, still permit the exchange of moist air through their pores and should not be used. It is false economy to buy improper wrappings and containers, for if the moisture is taken from the foods in zero storage that are not carefully wrapped in moisture-vaporproof wrappings, or if the covering becomes torn during storage, the foods will be dry and of inferior quality. They will lose flavor, color, and food value.

Loss of moisture in frozen foods also means that the food is exposed to the oxygen in the air. Exposure to oxygen hastens the rancidity of fats. Grayish-white spots are apt to develop on the surface of meat which is inadequately protected. This is known as "freezer burn." Actually, the meat has not been burned at all; rather, it has been robbed of its moisture, or dehydrated, and oxidation has taken place. Though still edible, the meat is definitely of poor quality.

Besides resisting the passage of moisture-vapor and protecting the food from contact with the air inside the freezer, packaging materials must protect the food from leakage and the possibility of an exchange of flavors between one food and another. Fish, butter, cheese, and pastries are all stored side by side, and if an exchange of flavors is permitted, the results could be disastrous. Butter, for example, will pick up other flavors if given the slightest opportunity.

Packaging materials should be odorless, tasteless, flexible, and easy to handle, seal, and label. They should be strong enough to stand considerable handling without cracking, durable enough to resist puncturing by bones or sharp edges, and they must not become brittle at zero temperature.

Packaging materials should be relatively inexpensive and economical of storage space. Square or rectangular cartons stack easily and use a minimum of space. They are available in pint and quart sizes, and you should select the size that is most suited to your family needs. A quart container will give you 6 to 8 servings of a vegetable or 8 to 10 servings of fruit. One cubic foot of freezer space will house about 24 rectangular or square cartons, but only 16 round or slope-sided cartons.

Briefly, here are the points to consider when you are shopping for packaging materials. They

1. Must be moisture-vaporproof to protect the food from contact with the air inside the cabinet and loss of moisture, flavor, and odor.

2. Must protect the food from leakage and the possibility of an exchange of flavors.

3. Must be easy to handle and seal.

4. Must be strong and durable.

5. Should be fairly inexpensive.

6. Should use a minimum of storage space.

Sheet wrappings

Aluminum foil is easy to use, as it may be fitted snugly around the food, expelling the excess air, and does not require taping or heat-sealing. When two surfaces of aluminum foil are pressed tightly together, the package is sealed. It punctures easily and must be protected by an outside wrap, but it is excellent for wrapping roasts, poultry, and large fish.

Moisture-vaporproof Cellophane needs an overwrap to protect it from puncturing. It must be soft and pliable. Should it become brittle from age, place it in the refrigerator for 46 hours and it will regain its pliability. It may be used to wrap steaks, chops, poultry, and fish.

Pliofilm is heavier and sturdier than Cellophane. It is excellent for wrapping irregular-shaped foods and makes a handsome, air-free package because of its rubberlike quality. It needs a protective covering.

Polyethylene is a plastic film that will stand more handling than either Cellophane or Pliofilm. It is particularly strong and pliable and needs no overwrap.

Saran is an excellent new transparent plastic film that clings closely to food, eliminating air pockets. It is moisture-vaporproof, pliable, strong, and reusable.

Laminated papers are made of two sheets of different materials held together by a flexible adhesive. It may be Pliofilm laminated to aluminum foil, or Glassine or Cellophane laminated to heavy paper. The lamination makes the paper moisture-vaporproof. Laminated papers are perfect for wrapping roasts. The packages may be tied simply with string and need no outer protection.

Containers

Flat, top-opening, heavily waxed paper cartons with a moisture-vaporproof liner or overwrap are ideal for such vegetables as asparagus, corn-on-the-cob, and broccoli. They are also good for chops, hamburgers, croquettes, fish filets, and disjointed poultry. They are easy to stack and freeze faster because they are flat.

Leakproof paraffined containers are good for moist foods, soups, stews, sauces, and semiliquid foods such as butter and ice cream. The square ones save storage space.

Plastic containers are also liquid-tight and easy to fill. They are excellent for ground meats, butter, ice cream, and semisolid foods that can be pressed into them, eliminating air pockets. They are especially suitable for leftovers and although they are fairly expensive compared with other cartons on the market, they can be used indefinitely.

Glass freezer jars have been especially designed to withstand extreme changes in temperature. They have wide mouths and tapered sides to facilitate the removal of the frozen contents. The rustproof metal screw caps make a leakproof, airtight seal. The cap was ingeniously devised to bulge so the jar won't shatter in case insufficient headspace was left in the jar. Glass jars are excellent for fruit purées, juices, stews, soups, sauces, and leftovers, and they may be reused.

Additional basic packaging needs

Outer wrappings give added strength to packages and prevent the moisture-vaporproof coverings from tearing during storage.

Stockinette material is a tubular, loosely knitted cotton fabric that may be stretched over odd-shaped foods for added protection. *Locker paper, butcher paper, nylon stockings,* or *cheesecloth* may also be used as an overwrap. The great value of Polyethylene or laminated papers is that they do not need this extra protection.

You should also have on hand *locker tape*—a special tape which will hold even in the zero temperatures of your freezer for any length of time. Use it to seal edges, to cover accidental punctures, and to attach labels. You will need a *heat sealer* of some type and a *china marking pencil* which will label clearly all types of papers and cartons.

HOW TO PACKAGE FOODS FOR YOUR FREEZER

The way in which food is wrapped for the freezer is just as important in maintaining the quality of frozen food as the wrappings and containers that you buy. No matter how moisture-vapor-proof the wrappings may be, if they are carelessly sealed so that the air can get in and the moisture of the food can get out, you might just as well have never wrapped it at all.

Whether you are packaging in containers or wrapping in paper, exclude as much air as possible from the package. Air pockets between the food and the packaging material collect moisture from the food. Package in amounts that are suitable for your family needs. Label accurately and informatively and freeze at once.

The *drugstore fold* is the easiest way to make a close, tight wrap with any suitable sheet wrappings and is recommended for irregularly shaped foods such as poultry and cuts of meat. Place the food in the center of a large sheet of flexible, durable paper. Bring the ends of the paper above the meat and fold them over and over downward in a lock seal, drawing the paper as tightly to the food as possible. Then fold the ends, fitting and pressing the paper close to the food to avoid air pockets. Use low-temperature locker tape to seal the edges of the folds.

WRAPPING IS OF VITAL IMPORTANCE. The paper used must resist the passage of moisture-vapor and protect the food from contact with the air in the freezer. **Above:** The meat on the left was loosely wrapped with locker paper only. The meat on the right was correctly wrapped with moisture-vaporproof paper under the locker paper. **Below:** This shows the results of the roasts in frozen storage. On the left is the improperly wrapped roast. Note the shrinkage that has taken place and the grayish-white spots on the surface. This is known as "freezer burn." The meat has been robbed of its moisture and oxidation has destroyed the flavor and quality. On the right, the properly wrapped roast has retained full moisture, flavor, and quality.

TO SEAL HEAT-SEALING LINERS WITH AN IRON. Rest a wide strip of heavy cardboard on top of the carton. Fold the bag over it at a point where the seal can be made snugly against the contents, press out the air from the liner, and move the iron over the cardboard.

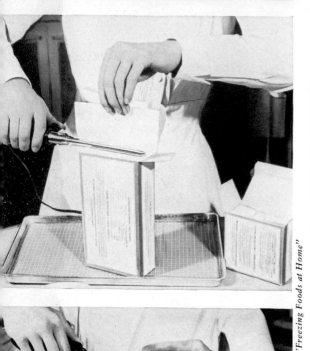

TO SEAL HEAT-SEALING LINERS WITH A CURLING IRON. Press out the air from the liner and seal the liner partway across close to the packaged food. Press out the remaining air and finish the seal. Then draw the iron upward toward the end of the bag. The sealing edge must be perfectly dry and clean to make a perfect heat seal.

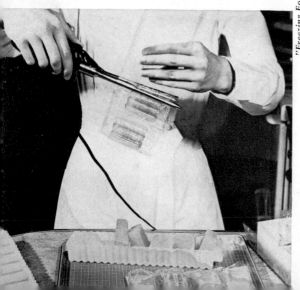

Eggs frozen in plastic ice cube trays can be taken from the tray and packaged in a thin bag of heat-sealing moisture-vapor-proof material. Use a lukewarm curling iron and seal directly across the bag, separating each frozen egg cube. A cube or two, depending on how much is needed, may be cut off and the bag returned to the freezer.

The *butcher wrap* is also used for the inner and outer wrap of sheet wrappings, or for a single wrap if laminated paper is used. Place the food diagonally across one corner of a large sheet of freezer paper. Fold over the sides and roll the package over and over until the food is completely covered. Wrap tightly to exclude the air and keep the package flat. Seal the edges carefully with low-temperature locker tape.

Folding cartons with heat-sealing liners. Open the moisture-vaporproof liner completely, including the corners, with the hand, and insert it in the opened carton. The use of a block of wood on which to form packages is a time saver. Fill the carton by means of a square funnel, or a tin can slightly flattened, to keep the top of the bag dry. The sealing edge must be perfectly dry and clean if you are going to have a perfect heat seal.

Press out the air from the liner and seal the liner partway across close down to the packaged food. Press out the remaining air and finish the seal. Then draw the iron upward toward the end of the bag. A wooden platform may be made to hold the package upright as you seal the liner. Another easy method of getting a seal close to the food is by resting a wide strip of heavy cardboard on top of the carton. Fold the bag over it at the point where the seal can be made snugly against the contents, press out the air from the liner, and move the iron over the cardboard. Use just enough heat and pressure to melt the plastic film or wax until it seals. Too much heat will scorch the liner and cause an imperfect seal.

Headspace must be left in packing liquid or semiliquid foods to allow for expansion during freezing and to prevent bulging of containers, leaking, or breakage of glass. The more liquid the product, the greater the expansion and the more headspace needed. Ideally, just enough space should be left so that the food will expand flush with the top, leaving no air pockets in the container, but this comes only by experience. In general, leave ½ inch headspace for most foods and 1 inch for juices. If ordinary glass jars are used for freezing, leave 1 inch in pints and 1½ inches in quarts.

Labeling. Every package in your freezer should be identified as to the kind of food, the weight or the number of servings, the date of storage, and the intended use of the contents.

Freeze immediately. The more quickly packaged foods get into your freezer the better they will be when cooked. Check your freezing compartment to make sure it can accommodate the amount of food you are preparing. Freeze at one time only the number of packages advised by the manufacturer of your freezer. Place the packages in contact with the freezer lining, with air space between them.

WHAT CAN YOU FREEZE?

Practically every type of food can be preserved by freezing except vegetables to be eaten raw and crisp, like lettuce, celery, radishes, cucumbers, tomatoes, cabbage, onions, and green peppers. Tomatoes may be frozen as juice or purée, or in ready-made dishes. Cabbage may be frozen and used as a cooked vegetable, but it will not retain its crispness.

Everything else freezes well—beef, lamb, pork, veal, and variety meats; chicken, ducks, turkeys, guinea hens, and geese; game birds, rabbits, squirrels, and venison; fish and shellfish; ice cream, sherbets, butter, cheese, and eggs; fruit juices and fruit purées; cakes, cookies, pies, puddings, bread, rolls, stews, soups, and ready-made dishes.

What should you freeze? Many books have been written about the home freezer and how to freeze everything from peanuts to porridge. Some authors discourse at length on how to conserve vegetables that are on the verge of spoiling and how many packages of sliced onions, minced onions, coarsely chopped onions, or quartered onions should be stored in your freezer to satisfy the requirements of a family of 4 or 6 or 8 for a period of 12 months. None of this makes a modicum of common sense and common sense is what you need when you own a home freezer.

Your freezer space is limited no matter what size you have, and if you are going to get the most from your freezer, every cubic inch must be strictly and wisely budgeted so that a variety of foods can be stored to satisfy the personal preferences of your entire family.

Your approach to daily living and where you live will naturally affect your decision as to what and how much you want to freeze. If you have a garden, naturally you will want to conserve the fruits and vegetables that cannot be eaten. Frozen fruits and vegetables are good, but they are never as good as when they are fresh, and for most city dwellers there is very little reason to freeze vegetables at all. Why freeze onions, turnips, beets, carrots, celery, green peppers? There is seldom a time throughout the year that these vegetables cannot be bought at your local vegetable store. Who would fill up her freezer with potatoes, just because she happened to have some spare time and felt in the mood to peel a peck? Certainly it makes sense to have a few packages of potato croquettes or French fried potatoes on hand. French fried onions are good too. But it makes no more sense to fill your freezer with potatoes or onions than to fill it with loaves of bread. Yet everyone should have a couple of loaves of French bread and a few packages of rolls and biscuits in the freezer for an emergency.

How difficult to resist filling the freezer with luscious frozen strawberries, raspberries, or peaches when they are in season! But resist you must, if you are going to use your frozen storage space to best advantage. It is so easy to fill the space in your freezer with the first products of spring—asparagus, peas, or strawberries—leaving scant room for the broccoli and spinach which follow later. A fine crop of late vegetables or fruits and no place to put them can cause regret. Don't forget that you can always buy fruits and vegetables, as you need them, meticulously prepared and properly packaged and frozen by reliable commercial freezers.

Also, just because you are the proud owner of a home freezer, don't lose sight of the fact that there *are* other excellent ways (and in certain specific instances *better* ways) to preserve foods. Don't forget to make some of your fruit into jams and jellies. Dill your cucumbers; use your peppers and cauliflower in chow-chow. Eat your fresh vegetables while they are in season. Buy the few frozen vegetables you need for winter use, or enjoy those underestimated root crops—beets, turnips, and parsnips—that keep so well in the cellar.

Don't hoard large quantities of meat and poultry in your freezer. There is little to be gained. Let your freezer work for you by keeping the space in constant use. Store wise quantities of meat and poultry. Eat the foods from your freezer, use them up quickly, plan a constant turnover, and make replacements with a fresh supply.

Fish, like vegetables, are never as good as when they are strictly fresh. You don't have to eat broiled lobster or oysters-on-the-half-shell every week. Eat them only when you can buy them alive at your fish market. Eat lots of fish when it is in season and store only as much as you will consume in three or four months.

Ready-cooked foods and entire meals may be frozen to have on hand at a moment's notice. Never make just a single recipe of your favorite dishes. Double or triple it and freeze what you don't eat that day for a quick and delicious meal next week.

It's just as easy to prepare and make chicken *cacciatore,* beef *bourguignonne,* fish chowder, or shrimp Newburg for 12 as it is for 4. This not only applies to stews, goulashes, casseroles, and soups, but to breads and pastries. Don't freeze sliced apples. Make 4 apple pies, bake and eat one, and freeze the other three.

So——

1. Be discriminating in the choice and selection of the foods you freeze. Freezer space is valuable—don't waste it.

2. Freeze only top-quality meats, poultry, and fish. Freezing does not improve anything; it merely maintains whatever quality the food had before it was frozen.

3. Freeze only the amount of food that can be used in a few months, and use your supply constantly. Don't hoard for that rainy day that may never come.

4. Plan a constant turnover. No food improves with long storage and quality in some cases is lost after only a few months.

5. Save enough room for leftovers and for ready-made dishes.

PLANNING AND INVENTORY

Anticipate your fruit and vegetable needs

Plan in advance what you are going to freeze and how much, depending on the preferences of your family, to avoid overloading with the first crops of the season. Peak seasons for fruits and vegetables vary from one state to another. In New York State the seasons run approximately as follows:

May: Asparagus, rhubarb

June: Asparagus, sweet cherries, spinach, strawberries, turnip greens

July: Beets, blackberries, blueberries, carrots, sour cherries, sweet cherries, currants, gooseberries, kohlrabi, peas, raspberries

August: Apples, green-shell beans, snap beans, beets, blackberries, blueberries, carrots, chard, eggplant, peaches, peppers, turnips

September: Apples, Lima beans, carrots, chard, sweet corn, cranberries, peaches, peppers, plums, prunes, winter squash, turnips, soybeans

October: Apples, broccoli, Brussels sprouts, cauliflower, cranberries, kale, soybeans

November: Broccoli, Brussels sprouts, kale

Planning your frozen meat supply

A supply of meat can be put into the home freezer at any time of the year. The greatest supply, however, is available at the time when prices are lowest, normally during the late fall, winter, and early spring months. This is the time when farmers usually butcher. The harvest has been brought in and farmers have more time for butchering from November 15 to March 15. Also, at this time the weather is cold and the carcasses can be quickly chilled.

The logical way to fill the freezer with meat is once in the fall and again in early spring. Stocking up on meats only twice a year leaves more space for the seasonable fruits, vegetables, and poultry.

Planning your poultry supply

Poultry is in season most of the year, but from May to November the supply is at its greatest:

Broilers—May to July

Fryers—June to August

Roasters and *fowl*—June to November

Arrange the foods in your freezer systematically

A well organized freezer holds more packages. It may take a little more time than just throwing packages in haphazardly, but an orderly freezer is much more convenient to use. Bad planning often results in a scramble through the entire contents of the freezer in order to find a certain package, or it may mean that the last frozen are the first to be used, leaving some packages deep within the freezer much longer than they should be stored for best quality. Group the same kinds of foods together, assigning certain sections to vegetables, fruits, meats, poultry, and ready-cooked dishes. Place newly frozen packages at the bottom or back of their section so that the older ones will be the first used.

Keep a running inventory

An elaborate inventory is not necessary, but some system that will keep you informed at all times as to what and how much of the different foods you have on hand is absolutely essential if you are going to get the best use from your freezer.

An inventory

1. Helps you keep a balanced assortment of foods in your freezer.
2. Helps you plan your menus.
3. Reminds you to use up packages that might otherwise be held too long and thus lose quality.
4. Warns you that certain items should be replenished.

Some like a series of recipe cards in a file box or a loose-leaf binder, each item with its own page or card. I prefer a good-sized slate blackboard and a piece of chalk. This is probably the simplest and most effective method of keeping an up-to-date record of the contents of your freezer, but make sure you keep it away from mischievous children!

Here are two examples of simple inventories:

VEGETABLES	DATE	IN	OUT	BALANCE
Asparagus	5/10/53	6	1–1–1–1	~~6~~ ~~5~~ ~~4~~ ~~3~~ 2
Spinach	6/4/53	6		6

MEAT

Porterhouse (for 4)	11/6/53	6	1–1	~~6~~ ~~5~~ 4
Round Steak (for 6)	12/15/53	4	1	~~4~~ 3
Venison Roast (7 pounds)	11/2/53	2		2

POULTRY

Ducks (6 pounds)	5/12/53	6		6
Chicken Fryers (3 pounds)	6/3/53	12	1–1	~~12~~ ~~11~~ 10

Instead of listing the date on which the food was frozen, you might prefer to list the date by which the food should be used for top quality. In this way you don't have to do any mental gymnastics every time you review your inventory.

	USE BY	NO. OF PACKAGES
Sausage Meat	3/15/53	~~8~~ ~~7~~ ~~6~~ ~~5~~ 4

HOW LONG CAN FOODS BE STORED AT ZERO?

Many people have the misconception that a freezer preserves food indefinitely. *This is not true.* Freezing simply slows down the destructive action of the organisms that cause food spoilage—it does not destroy these organisms. The length of time that a food can be stored in your freezer without losing quality and flavor depends on the particular food, and the maximum storage times given throughout this book should be taken seriously if you are going to get the greatest enjoyment from your frozen foods.

Certainly no food should be kept longer than from one growing season to another, but most foods should be kept for much shorter periods. Your freezer should not be treated like a revered, almost untouchable hope chest. It should be made an active source of your daily food supply.

A great deal of research and experimentation has been done by the manufacturers of home freezers, by the United States Department of Agriculture and by the many State colleges in order to determine the maximum storage life of various foods. As a result, we have learned that many factors affect the keeping qualities of food and that all foods do not have the same storage life.

We know that the variety and the maturity of fruits and vegetables and the speed and care given to them in their preparation is important.

We know that the proper scalding of vegetables is vital to their frozen life.

We have discovered that bacon and salt pork must not be kept in the freezer very long because the salt used in curing these meats accelerates the development of rancidity in the fat.

We know that ground and sliced meats have a relatively short storage life, because a greater amount of surface is exposed to the destructive chemical process of oxidation. Fat is the bad actor in zero storage and for this reason fat meat such as pork and fatty fish should not be kept longer than their recommended storage period.

A DOZEN BASIC RULES FOR HOME FREEZING

1. Select top quality. You get nothing better out of your freezer than you put in. Freezing retains quality, but it does not improve it. Meats should be top grade and properly aged; poultry should be young and tender; fish, fresh. Vegetables should be full-flavored, young, and firm; picked at their peak of perfection. Fruits are right

when they are ready to eat out of hand. *Don't waste freezer space with inferior foods.*

2. Choose varieties of fruits and vegetables best adapted to freezing. Some freeze better than others. The varieties vary according to locality, so consult your local State college.

3. Work quickly. Two hours from field to freezer is a good rule.

4. Prepare foods carefully.

5. Follow directions. The instructions in this book are the result of the latest and most authoritative research on freezing combined with personal experience. *Vegetables must be scalded.*

6. Freeze small batches at a time. Don't overestimate your energy. Handle only the amount that can be processed quickly and don't burden your freezer with too many unfrozen packages at one time.

7. Chill foods before freezing. Scalded vegetables should be instantly cooled in ice water. Meat, fish, and poultry should be chilled to make sure that all the body heat has been dispersed.

8. Wrap snugly in moisture-vaporproof materials and seal perfectly. All foods must be protected from air, the escape of moisture, and an exchange of flavors.

9. Label every package intelligently and informatively.

10. Freeze packaged foods immediately.

11. Keep a running inventory.

12. Observe recommended storage periods. Plan a constant turnover of the contents of your freezer so that no food will be given the opportunity to lose quality and flavor.

CAN YOU REFREEZE FOODS?

In general, refreezing is not a good idea, as the food suffers a loss of flavor and quality. Completely thawed poultry, meats, and non-acid vegetables, which are subject to attack by harmful bacteria should not be refrozen. Fruits and acid vegetables, however, are not prey to such bacteria and may be safely refrozen.

Any food only partially thawed may be tucked away again at zero temperature without a qualm.

COMMERCIALLY FROZEN FOODS

Buy only top-quality foods from reliable dealers to store in your freezer. Don't be swayed by sensational "bargains" that are offered to you, for no food in the world is a "bargain" if it is of poor and inferior quality. Beware of any so-called "food plan" that promises to fill your freezer (providing you buy it from the distributors who organized the "food plan") with foods at such a low cost that the savings for you will more than pay for the cost of buying and operating your home freezer. Before you enter into such a scheme, better check with your Better Business Bureau.

Every month the selection of commercially frozen foods increases. Many cooked dishes, and even complete meals, are appearing in the stores. Such items are crab flakes, shrimp creole, chicken pie, chicken à la King, fried chicken, lamb stew, chow mein, oyster stew, clam chowder, onion soup, spaghetti sauce, hors d'oeuvres, fruit pies, cakes, and rolls are available.

When you buy frozen foods instead of fresh, you must consider the cost of food per serving and not the cost of food per pound. Remember that frozen foods are meticulously prepared and properly packaged for you. There is no waste. Frozen foods, on this basis, are not as expensive as they might seem. The following table from the Quick Frozen Food Association of Chicago shows the equivalent weights of frozen and fresh foods.

TABLE OF EQUIVALENTS

VEGETABLES	FROZEN EQUIVALENT TO:	FRESH
Asparagus	12 oz.	1 lb. 10 oz.
Green Beans	10 oz.	14 oz.
Wax Beans	10 oz.	14 oz.
Broccoli	10 oz.	1 lb. 6 oz.
Brussels Sprouts	10 oz.	1 lb. 4 oz.

VEGETABLES	FROZEN EQUIVALENT TO:	FRESH
Cauliflower	10 oz.	Med. Head
Cut Corn	12 oz.	6 ears
Lima Beans	12 oz.	2 lbs.
Peas	12 oz.	2 lbs.
Peas and Carrots	12 oz.	2 lbs.
Mixed Vegetables	12 oz.	2 lbs.
Spinach	14 oz.	2 lbs. 8 oz.
Squash	16 oz.	1 lb. 6 oz.

POULTRY

Broilers and Fryers	2 lbs.	3 lbs. Undrawn
Roasters	3 lbs.	4 lbs. Undrawn
Fowl	2½ lbs.	3½ lbs. Undrawn
Turkeys	9 lbs.	12 lbs. Undrawn

FISH

Cod and Haddock	1 lb.	3 lbs. Whole
Mackerel	1 lb.	1¾ lbs. Whole
Flounder (Sole)	1 lb.	4 lbs. Whole
Ocean Perch	1 lb.	5 lbs. Whole

CHAPTER TWO

How to freeze meat and large game

No other method of preservation retains the fresh taste and texture of meat and game as well as freezing. Whether you buy your meat or slaughter it yourself; whether you dress it yourself or have your butcher do it for you, you can enjoy better year-round eating and greater variety in your meals.

A home freezer with a good supply of the various types and cuts of meat is of course a great boon to those who live far from a meat market. It is also a blessing to us who earn our daily bread five days a week and were mightily wearied of those evening stops at the butcher to pick up a steak or some chops. To everyone, a supply of meat in the freezer means security, the satisfaction of knowing that meat, the most important part of any meal, is at hand and waiting to be cooked.

All meats, including specialties such as sweetbreads, heart, liver, and brains, freeze well. It is economical to buy a large portion of a carcass for use throughout the year, or to buy specially priced cuts to be enjoyed months later. Often the opportunity arises for the "city dweller" with limited freezer space to buy special meat or a specific cut of meat from the butcher at a real bargain. But any meat you buy for your freezer should be grade A quality, properly aged, cut, and boned, and packaged in the size most convenient for your family.

Some meats are slightly more tender after freezing than when fresh. This does not mean that inferior grades of meat become choice after freezing. Freezing seals in the original quality and flavor, it does not improve it. If you fill your freezer with inferior, tough meat, it will still be tough and dry and of poor quality when taken out.

SELECTING MEAT FOR YOUR FREEZER

Whether you purchase retail cuts, or buy an animal or portion of a carcass to be dressed for you, or do your own slaughtering and dressing, choose prime meats, moderately fat and well finished.

A good animal is thickly fleshed in the ribs, loin, and hindquarters. An ample layer of fat not only protects the lean meat from drying out during the freezing period, but adds flavor when the meat is cooked. Too much fat, however, should be avoided, as fat oxidizes quickly and rancidity is likely to occur. Veal rarely has surplus fat and is an exception to the general rule. The less tender portions of an animal should be cut and packaged for braising or stewing, or ground for Hamburgers and meat loaves.

SLAUGHTERING

It is a wise precaution to have a veterinarian inspect animals to insure that only healthy ones are slaughtered for food.

If you live on a farm and have proper equipment and cool, clean, adequate space, you will probably do your own slaughtering. Detailed information can be obtained from your local extension office of the United States Department of Agriculture, but unless you have had experience it is wiser by far to enlist the services of an expert butcher. A good deal of fine meat can be spoiled when amateurs slaughter animals. Most locker plants not only sell meats, but have skilled services for slaughtering, butchering, chilling, aging, cutting, wrapping, and freezing.

On the farm, slaughtering is done from late fall to early spring, when the weather is cool enough to chill the carcass quickly and thoroughly. In warm months, unless adequate refrigeration is available, the meat will spoil at outdoor temperatures.

Feed should be withheld for 18 to 24 hours before animals are slaughtered, but plenty of water should be available. Slaughtering should be done in the evening so the carcasses can be hung in the cold night air, and only at a time when the weather is expected to remain at or a little below 40° F. The temperature should not rise above this; neither should it drop below the freezing point. The ideal temperature for slaughtering is between 33 and 38° F.

CHILLING CARCASSES

Prompt and thorough chilling of slaughtered animals under sanitary conditions is imperative to prevent spoilage and to protect the meat from contact with undesirable odors. The body temperature of freshly slaughtered meat is around 100° F. and it must be reduced to between 33 and 38° F. within 24 hours.

Meat cut from warm carcasses is soft and will not hold its shape, resulting in ragged, unattractive cuts. If more than one carcass is hung, room must be left between them so that the air can circulate as the carcasses cool. If the removal of body heat is not prompt and thorough, destructive molds, yeasts, and bacteria multiply with such speed that the flavor of the meat will be ruined and the flesh may become unfit for use. It must be kept in mind when cooling meat that warm flesh is most receptive to such odors as mildew, paint, and disinfectant.

A beef carcass should be split in half and washed thoroughly in plenty of lukewarm water. It will take 24 hours at 34° F. for the carcass of a 1000-pound steer to cool to an internal temperature of 38° F. at its thickest part. A clean skewer-type thermometer should be inserted in the thickest muscle to determine the internal temperature, for if the temperature is reduced to only 40° F., instead of 38° F., this small difference of just two degrees is apt to result in souring at the hip bone.

Hogs, calves, lambs, and mutton also require about 24 hours' chilling at 34° F.

Rapid chilling of pork at temperatures between 33 and 38° F. is most essential. Pork may sour in 12 hours if it is hung in a warm temperature, or if the carcasses are allowed to overlap so the cold air cannot circulate around them. Many hams are lost in curing because the hogs were slaughtered when the weather was too warm and the carcasses were not quickly and efficiently chilled to 38° F. or lower. To speed the chilling, the warm hogs should be split, the internal organs removed, and the leaf lard pulled out. Should the weather be below freezing, the carcasses should be wrapped in sheets and hung in a shed to protect them from freezing. And hang they must. Never lay them on the ground or floor.

The heavier and fatter the hog, the more carefully it must be handled. Rapid chilling cannot be overemphasized, but at the same time it must be thorough. Test the internal temperature of the large pieces of meat, such as the hams, with a meat thermometer. If the temperature is above 38° F., the carcass should be cut and the large pieces spread out during a second night to complete the chilling.

Freshly killed game needs even quicker attention than domestic animals, for spoilage starts immediately in the area of the wound. Large game, such as deer, moose, or antelope, should be bled promptly after they are killed and eviscerated. The body cavity must be wiped out with a clean cloth, but it should not be washed. If it is raining or snowing, the carcass should be protected with canvas or burlap. If the weather is warm, the carcass must be covered with a sheet or cheesecloth to protect it from insects.

AGING

Young animals about 1 year old, such as pork and veal, do not need aging. They should be cut and packaged directly after cooling —especially pork, for pork fat becomes rancid quickly.

Variety meats, such as heart, liver, tongue, kidneys, and brains, should be chilled, cleaned, packaged, and frozen immediately.

Beef, lamb, mutton, and large game are improved in flavor and texture if they are allowed to age in a well-ventilated room at temperatures between 32 and 38° F. for 5 to 10 days.

Humidity is as important as temperature in the aging room. If the humidity is too low, the air will draw moisture from the meat and the carcass will become dry. If the humidity is too high, above 90 per cent, bacterial growth is apt to take place and the flesh will become slimy.

Aging breaks down the connective tissues and makes the meat more tender, but the length of time depends on the kind, quality, and size of the carcass, and an expert should be consulted.

The following aging periods are only approximate:

Beef	5 to 8 days
Large game	5 to 14 days
Mutton	2 to 3 days
Lamb	1 to 3 days

CUTTING AND BONING MEAT

Once again, this phase of preparing meat for the freezer is no job for the novice. You should employ an expert butcher. Most locker plants employ meat cutters or can direct you to one. Usually the charge for such services is reasonable, and it is good economics, in the over-all picture, for someone trained in the profession can cut meat into uniform shape and thickness and can get the greatest number of desirable cuts.

It is wise, however, to direct the cutter as he works so that you will have the cuts which experience has taught you are most practical for your family.

Consider the size of your family and have the meat cut in family-sized portions. Give thought to your preference in cooking and have the less desirable cuts, such as brisket, plate, and shank, cut into cubes for braising, or have them ground for meat loaves or patties. Consider the number of guests you entertain in your home and you will want to have some attractive guest-sized cuts. Have your steaks cut good and thick. Thin steaks tend to dry out in several months' zero storage and also in cooking. Package roasts, chops, and steaks in meal-sized portions, planning some extra-thick, succulent steaks, some choice roasts, a few double lamp chops, and so on, for special occasions.

Boning meat has become popular during the past few years for several reasons. Boned and rolled meat requires less space in your freezer, generally saving 25 per cent space, and in the case of lamb, it saves as much as 50 per cent. Less dehydration and oxidation can take place because of the snug, compact wrapping possible around the smooth surface of the rolled meat, which has no protruding bones to rupture the wrapping. When a roast is boned and rolled and tied, it may be cut into family-sized portions and when cooked it may be carved more easily than a roast containing the bones. The bones may be used to make soup stock, and the stock may be frozen in convenient-sized packages. The only disadvantage to boning meat is that it takes time and therefore increases the cost.

To help you direct the expert who cuts your meat, you must know and understand what he is doing. The following charts, given through the courtesy of the National Live Stock and Meat Board, show clearly the standard cuts made from a carcass or a portion of a carcass.

You will want to know too, if you purchase either a whole animal or a portion of one, how many pounds of meat, cut and trimmed, ready to be wrapped and frozen, you are going to realize from your purchase.

Cutting beef

APPROXIMATE YIELD OF A WHOLE CARCASS

Live weight	750 pounds
Whole carcass	420
Dressed weight	338

TRIMMED CUTS FROM A WHOLE CARCASS

Steaks and oven roasts	40% of carcass weight, or 172 pounds
Pot roasts	20% of carcass weight, or 83 pounds
Stews and ground meat	20% of carcass weight, or 83 pounds
Total	80% of carcass weight, or 338 pounds

BEEF CUTS AND HOW TO COOK THEM

Retail Cuts   **Wholesale Cuts**   **Retail Cuts**

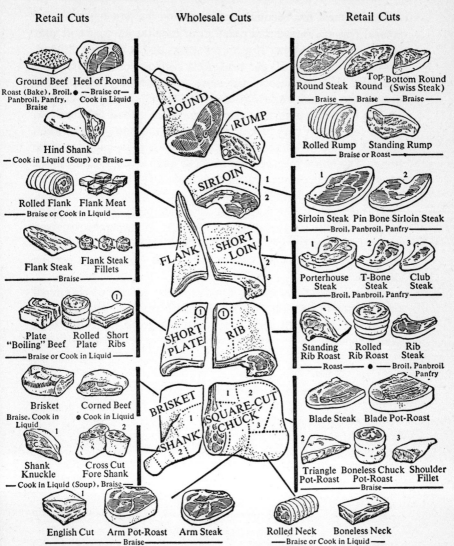

Ground Beef   Heel of Round
Roast (Bake), Broil, ● ─Braise or─
Panbroil, Panfry,   Cook in Liquid
Braise

Hind Shank
─ Cook in Liquid (Soup) or Braise ─

Rolled Flank   Flank Meat
─ Braise or Cook in Liquid ─

Flank Steak   Flank Steak Fillets
─ Braise ─

Plate   Rolled   Short
"Boiling" Beef   Plate   Ribs
─ Braise or Cook in Liquid ─

Brisket   Corned Beef
Braise, Cook in   ● Cook in Liquid
Liquid

Shank   Cross Cut
Knuckle   Fore Shank
─ Cook in Liquid (Soup), Braise ─

English Cut   Arm Pot-Roast   Arm Steak
─ Braise ─

ROUND   RUMP

SIRLOIN

FLANK   SHORT LOIN

SHORT PLATE   RIB

BRISKET   SQUARE-CUT CHUCK
SHANK

Rolled Neck   Boneless Neck
─ Braise or Cook in Liquid ─

Round Steak   Top   Bottom Round
Round   (Swiss Steak)
─ Braise ─   ─ Braise ─   ─ Braise ─

Rolled Rump   Standing Rump
─ Braise or Roast ─

Sirloin Steak   Pin Bone Sirloin Steak
─ Broil, Panbroil, Panfry ─

Porterhouse   T-Bone   Club
Steak   Steak   Steak
─ Broil, Panbroil, Panfry ─

Standing   Rolled   Rib
Rib Roast   Rib Roast   Steak
─ Roast ─   ●   Broil, Panbroil Panfry

Blade Steak   Blade Pot-Roast

Triangle   Boneless Chuck   Shoulder
Pot-Roast   Pot-Roast   Fillet
─ Braise ─

Courtesy of National Live Stock and Meat Board

FOREQUARTERS WILL YIELD

Steaks and oven roasts	25% of carcass weight, or 55 pounds
Pot roasts	32% of carcass weight, or 70 pounds
Stews and ground meat	27% of carcass weight, or 59 pounds
Total	84% of carcass weight, or 184 pounds

HINDQUARTERS WILL YIELD

Steaks and oven roasts	58% of carcass weight, or 117 pounds
Stews and ground meat	18% of carcass weight, or 37 pounds
Total	76% of carcass weight, or 154 pounds

The approximate loss of 82 pounds between the weight of the carcass and the dressed meat is due to normal shrinkage, the loss of hide, fat, and meat trimmings, and the bones which are removed before the cuts are trimmed, and also the liver, tongue, and heart.

How the animal is cut depends a good deal on whether the animal was reasonably young, well fed, and well bred. If so, the rib and top round are satisfactory for steaks, and the rib and arm side of the chuck are usually tender enough to be oven-roasted. If the animal is old and thin, all these sections should be prepared for braising rather than roasting or broiling.

The best cuts for roasting are made from the rib sections of the carcass and the roast cut from the prime ribs, the standing rib roast, is a choice one. The bones may be removed, the meat rolled compactly and tied at one-inch intervals with string. The roll may then be cut at intervals parallel to the string into family- or guest-sized portions. The bones may also be removed from the rump, chuck, flank, plate, and neck to save freezer space.

Choice steaks cut from the loin, such as sirloin, porterhouse, T-bone, and club steaks, should not be boned. And before the round is sliced into steaks, it should be separated into three distinct parts in order to yield steaks of uniform tenderness. These parts are the top of the round, which is the most tender, the bottom of the round, and the heel of the round. The steaks from both the bottom and top of the round should be sliced crosswise against the grain.

The less tender cuts from the shank, brisket, plate, flank, and neck are usually best when boned and ground or cubed for stews and casseroles. But save a slice of plate for boiled beef and get a pot roast from the arm.

Be sure to form ground meat for Hamburgers into patties before freezing, so that they do not have to be thawed but can be broiled or sautéed directly from the freezer. One pound of ground meat, free of gristle and too much fat, makes 4 medium-sized Hamburgers.

The heart and tongue may be frozen whole. The liver may be frozen whole or sliced before freezing.

Cutting lamb

APPROXIMATE YIELD OF A WHOLE CARCASS

Live weight	85 pounds
Whole carcass	41 pounds
Dressed weight	38 pounds

TRIMMED CUTS FROM A WHOLE CARCASS

Legs, chops, shoulders	75% of carcass weight, or 31 pounds
Breast and stew	15% of carcass weight, or 7 pounds
Total	90% of carcass weight, or 38 pounds

A leg of lamb is usually cut into two roasts. The best is the lower part, called "The Frenched Roast," which has part of the leg bone extending beyond the flesh. The upper part of the leg, called "The American Leg," is easier to wrap for the freezer, for it has no protruding bone. The bone is cut below the hock well into the leg meat. Other lamb roasts are cut from the shoulder, loin, and breast. The loin of the leg yields three large chops, but the best chops

LAMB CUTS AND HOW TO COOK THEM

Retail Cuts	Wholesale Cuts	Retail Cuts

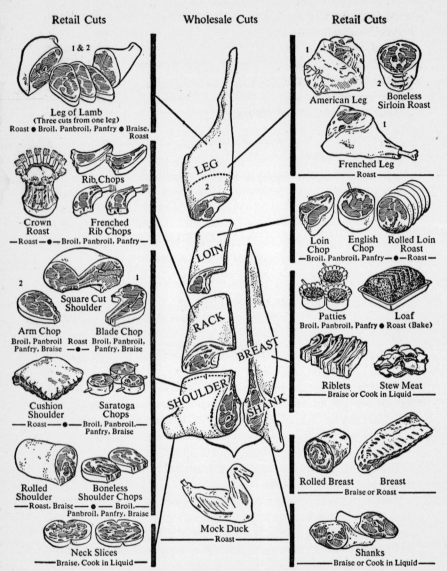

Leg of Lamb
(Three cuts from one leg)
Roast ● Broil, Panbroil, Panfry ● Braise, Roast

Rib Chops

Crown Roast
—Roast—

Frenched Rib Chops
●—Broil, Panbroil, Panfry—

Square Cut Shoulder

Arm Chop
Broil, Panbroil, Panfry, Braise

Blade Chop
Roast ●—● Broil, Panbroil, Panfry, Braise

Cushion Shoulder
—Roast—●—

Saratoga Chops
—Broil, Panbroil, Panfry, Braise

Rolled Shoulder
—Roast, Braise—●—

Boneless Shoulder Chops
—Broil, Panbroil, Panfry, Braise

Neck Slices
—Braise, Cook in Liquid—

LEG
LOIN
RACK
SHOULDER
BREAST
SHANK

Mock Duck
—Roast—

American Leg

Boneless Sirloin Roast

Frenched Leg
—Roast—

Loin Chop

English Chop

Rolled Loin Roast
—Broil, Panbroil, Panfry—●—Roast—

Patties
Broil, Panbroil, Panfry

Loaf
● Roast (Bake)

Riblets

Stew Meat
—Braise or Cook in Liquid—

Rolled Breast

Breast
—Braise or Roast—

Shanks
—Braise or Cook in Liquid—

Courtesy of National Live Stock and Meat Board

come from the loin itself. Rib chops are cut from the rack section, and Saratoga and shoulder chops come from the shoulder.

A crown roast of lamb is a difficult cut to wrap and takes up valuable space. If you want one for a special occasion, do not plan to store it for long, unless you have plenty of room in your freezer.

The breast meat may be rolled for braising, diced for stew, or ground for lamb loaf or patties.

Cutting pork

APPROXIMATE YIELD FROM A WHOLE CARCASS

Live weight	225 pounds
Whole carcass	176 pounds
*Dressed weight	124 pounds

In addition to the dressed weight, a whole carcass will yield about 27 pounds of rendered lard.

TRIMMED CUTS FROM A WHOLE CARCASS
Fresh hams, shoulders, bacon, jowls

	50% of carcass weight, or	90 pounds
Loins, ribs, sausage	20% of carcass weight, or	34 pounds
Total	70% of carcass weight, or	124 pounds

As with other meats, pork should be cut into meal-sized portions. Roasts are cut from the hams, lower loins, and shoulders. The shoulder may be divided into the bottom butt and top shoulder, and each part may be trimmed, boned, and rolled into roasts.

Chops—loin, rib, and butterfly—are all cut from the upper loin.

The hams are usually cured, but fresh hams may be sliced and frozen for fresh ham steaks.

Bacon and salt pork are cut from the belly and jowl for curing. Bacon may be frozen, but it does not adapt itself to freezing as well as fresh ham. If the bacon is sliced before it is frozen, it may dry and become rancid in a short time. If a supply of bacon must be frozen in order to preserve it, cut it into 1- or 2-pound slabs and wrap each slab in moisture-vaporproof paper. Take out a slab as it is needed, let it thaw, and then slice.

PORK CUTS AND HOW TO COOK THEM

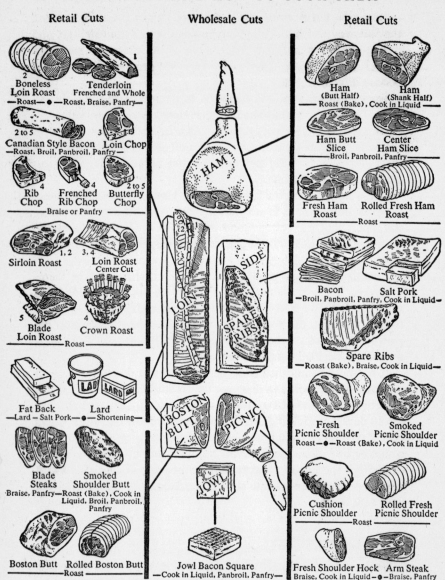

Retail Cuts   **Wholesale Cuts**   **Retail Cuts**

2 Boneless Loin Roast
—Roast—●—

1 Tenderloin
Frenched and Whole
—Roast, Braise, Panfry—

2 to 5 Canadian Style Bacon
—Roast, Broil, Panbroil, Panfry—

3 Loin Chop

4 Rib Chop

4 Frenched Rib Chop

2 to 5 Butterfly Chop
—Braise or Panfry—

1, 2 Sirloin Roast

3, 4 Loin Roast Center Cut

5 Blade Loin Roast

4 Crown Roast
—Roast—

Fat Back
—Lard - Salt Pork—●—

Lard
—Shortening—

Blade Steaks
—Braise, Panfry—

Smoked Shoulder Butt
—Roast (Bake), Cook in Liquid, Broil, Panbroil, Panfry—

Boston Butt

Rolled Boston Butt
—Roast—

HAM

LOIN

SIDE

SPARE RIBS

BOSTON BUTT

PICNIC

JOWL

Jowl Bacon Square
—Cook in Liquid, Panbroil, Panfry—

Ham (Butt Half)

Ham (Shank Half)
—Roast (Bake), Cook in Liquid—

Ham Butt Slice

Center Ham Slice
—Broil, Panbroil, Panfry—

Fresh Ham Roast

Rolled Fresh Ham Roast
—Roast—

Bacon

Salt Pork
—Broil, Panbroil, Panfry, Cook in Liquid—

Spare Ribs
—Roast (Bake), Braise, Cook in Liquid—

Fresh Picnic Shoulder
—Roast—●—

Smoked Picnic Shoulder
—Roast (Bake), Cook in Liquid—

Cushion Picnic Shoulder

Rolled Fresh Picnic Shoulder
—Roast—

Fresh Shoulder Hock
—Braise, Cook in Liquid—●—

Arm Steak
—Braise, Panfry—

Courtesy of National Live Stock and Meat Board

Spareribs, cut from the belly, take up a lot of freezer space, but they are well worth it. They keep beautifully in frozen storage, and if they are packaged flat, layer upon layer, with two sheets of freezer paper between the layers, they will justify the space they occupy in your freezer.

Sausage meat is ground from the trimmings of the loin, blade, butts, bones, hams, and shoulders. It may be seasoned with salt, black pepper, red pepper, sage, or other herbs before it is frozen. Smoking prevents rancidity and drives off some of the moisture of the sausage meat. Fifty per cent fat and 50 per cent lean meat makes excellent sausage.

According to a recent letter from the United States Department of Agriculture, there is no information available to substantiate the report that the refrigeration of pork at 0° F. will insure the destruction of trichinella organisms that might be present in the meat.

Investigations have proven that once the trichinae larvae themselves reach a temperature of 0° F., they do not survive long and usually die in 24 hours. Once the larvae are embedded in the pork tissues, however, the period of refrigeration needed to destroy the parasites depends on the time required for all portions of the meat to reach a specified temperature.

It has been established that the trichinae are destroyed in pork not exceeding 6 inches in diameter that is subjected to −10° F. for a continuous period of 10 days, at −20° F. for 6 days, and at 5° F. for 20 days. Considering these facts, it seems most likely that small cuts of pork stored in a home freezer for a month or longer at 0° F. would be free of trichinae larvae, but until further experimentation determines the length of storage time for various cuts of pork, it would be wise to continue to cook all pork or foods containing pork until well done.

Cutting veal

Veal needs no aging. It must be chilled promptly and should be cut, packaged, and frozen immediately after the body temperature is reduced to 38° F.

The calf should weigh from 110 to 200 pounds, and the carcass will yield from 80 to 90 pounds of roasts, chops, and ground and stew meat. Veal is cut in a manner similar to beef. The hindquarter is cut into the round, rump, loin, and shank and yields cutlets, round steak, round roast, rump roast, rolled rump roast, sirloin steak, and loin and kidney chops. The forequarter is cut into shank, shoulder, breast, and rib and yields rib chops, rib roast or crown roast, blade and arm steaks and roasts, rolled shoulder, and ground and stew meats.

Cutting venison and other large game

Venison and other large game are cut in much the same way as beef or veal. Some States do not permit game to be stored for longer than 10 days, so you should familiarize yourself with the State laws in the locality in which you live. Consult your local game warden, or your State Conservation Department, for details.

HOW TO PACKAGE MEAT FOR THE FREEZER

Once meat has been cut, it should be packaged and frozen immediately. The meat should be shaped into its most compact form before it is wrapped to avoid air pockets. Trim off the excess fat to conserve freezer space and wrap carefully and tightly in heavy moisture-vaporproof paper, pressing the paper firmly against the meat, again forcing out the air pockets. The drugstore wrap is most effective. As the fold is formed, the paper can be pulled tightly against the meat. As the ends are folded, the air pockets can be pressed out. Seal the ends with acetate tape and label with the kind of cut, number of pieces, and date of freezing. Once packaged, freeze immediately, or the meat will lose moisture and juice rapidly.

Roasts and large cuts

Many of the wrapping materials now on the market protect roasts and large cuts of meat properly against loss of surface mois-

VEAL CUTS AND HOW TO COOK THEM

Retail Cuts   Wholesale Cuts   Retail Cuts

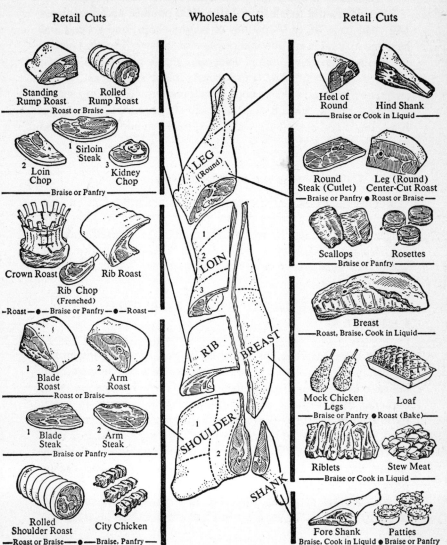

Standing Rump Roast   Rolled Rump Roast
— Roast or Braise —

2 Loin Chop   1 Sirloin Steak   3 Kidney Chop
— Braise or Panfry —

Crown Roast   Rib Roast
Rib Chop (Frenched)
— Roast — ● — Braise or Panfry — ● — Roast —

1 Blade Roast   2 Arm Roast
— Roast or Braise —

1 Blade Steak   2 Arm Steak
— Braise or Panfry —

Rolled Shoulder Roast   City Chicken
— Roast or Braise — ● — Braise, Panfry —

LEG (Round)

LOIN

RIB

BREAST

SHOULDER

SHANK

Heel of Round   Hind Shank
— Braise or Cook in Liquid —

Round Steak (Cutlet)   Leg (Round) Center-Cut Roast
— Braise or Panfry — ● Roast or Braise —

Scallops   Rosettes
— Braise or Panfry —

Breast
— Roast, Braise, Cook in Liquid —

Mock Chicken Legs   Loaf
— Braise or Panfry — ● Roast (Bake) —

Riblets   Stew Meat
— Braise or Cook in Liquid —

Fore Shank   Patties
Braise, Cook in Liquid ● Braise or Panfry

Courtesy of National Live Stock and Meat Board

ture, oxidation, and rancidity. It is unwise to economize on wrappings for meat. If there are any protruding bones, pad them before wrapping the meat to prevent the bones from breaking through.

If Pliofilm, Polyethylene, Saran, or aluminum foil is used, a stockinette overwrap should be pulled snugly around the paper to protect it against tearing. Tie a knot in the stockinette tightly against the roast. Cut off and tie the end of the stockinette in a knot. Attach a tag or label. If one of the laminated papers is used, no overwrap is necessary. Wrap tightly. The package should be smooth and firm when it is finished.

Steaks and chops

Package the number of steaks, chops, or cutlets that you will need for one meal in each package with two pieces of freezer paper between them, so that they can be separated when you are ready to use them without first thawing the entire package. Keep the meat flat as you wrap it, packing the chops or steaks tightly together in neat, regular layers. Top-opening cartons stack well and conserve freezer space.

When frozen steaks or chops can be readily separated you may, if you wish, cook them from the frozen state without thawing. Or, if you do not need the amount of chops or steaks that you anticipated when you packaged them, one or more can be removed and the package then resealed and placed again in the freezer.

Ground meat

Ground meat should never be refrozen; therefore it should be packaged in the right amount for a specific recipe. Pack the amount of ground meat you will need for a casserole firmly in a top-opening carton, pressing out any air pockets. Make meat loaves all ready to pop in the oven, wrap in moisture-vaporproof paper, and seal completely. Form ground meat into patties and pack the patties in layers, separating the layers with two sheets of freezer paper. Or each patty may be wrapped separately and packed in a top-opening carton. Either way the patties may be easily separated for cooking directly from the frozen state, or a few may be cooked and the others returned to the freezer. Overwrap the cartons and heat-seal the edges and ends.

Meats for braising

Wrap large roasts for braising or boiling in the same manner as oven roasts. Cubed stew meat should be pressed firmly into rigid containers or cartons.

Variety meats

Prepare variety meats such as liver, tongue, heart, and kidneys as soon as they are chilled. Liver may be cut into slices of the desired thickness, the slices separated with two sheets of freezer paper, and packaged flat. Hearts may also be sliced. Variety meats should not be stored longer than 4 to 6 months, with the exception of liver, which should be stored from 2 to 4 months only.

Smoked meats

The keeping qualities of hams and bacon at zero temperature depend entirely on how well the meat was processed and the type of cure, but generally they should not be kept longer than a few months. It is especially important that these meats be wrapped tightly to prevent their drying out and to prohibit the transfer of flavor to other foods. Freeze bacon in 1- or 2-pound slabs rather than slices and slice it after it is thawed.

If hams and bacon are fully cured and hung in a cool, dry room, they will keep for as long as 6 months, so there is little reason to occupy freezer space with them. However, the flavor of hams and bacon that are only mildly cured is delicate and delicious, and a mild cure may be used if these products are to be frozen.

Sausage

Spices and other seasonings such as black and red pepper, sage, and other herbs actually retard rancidity in sausage meat, but salt

speeds up oxidation in any meat. The sausage may be completely
seasoned, or the salt may be omitted and added before or during
cooking. If salt is added, plan to use the sausage in a short time.
Without salt, sausage meat may be safely stored in your freezer
for as long as 6 months. Package in the same way as ground meat.

Bones and trimmings may be frozen for pet food, or they may be
cooked with vegetables and seasonings for soup stock. Package
stock in cartons, allowing 1 inch headspace. For a small quantity
to use in casseroles, stews, and sautées, cook the stock until it is reduced to one half or less its original quantity and freeze in ice-cube
trays. When frozen, the cubes of frozen stock may be wrapped individually and several put into a bag or carton.

Label intelligently

It takes only a few seconds to write on the wrapper the type of
meat, the number of servings, the date, and whether it is to be used
for a specific purpose or a favorite recipe.

Keep meat cool during and after wrapping

If meat is wrapped in a warm room, it should be chilled in the
refrigerator before it is frozen. Freeze only as much at one time as
can be solidly frozen within 24 hours.

COOKING FROZEN MEAT

Frozen meat may be cooked when solidly frozen, when partially
thawed, or when completely thawed.

When meat is thawed there is a considerable loss of juice and
therefore flavor and for this reason the ideal method of roasting
frozen meat is to place it in the oven immediately after it is removed
from the freezer and unwrapped. An additional 15 to 20 minutes'
cooking time per pound must be allowed, as the meat must defrost
as it cooks. In order to have frozen meat cooked to perfection, insert a meat thermometer in the thickest part as soon as the meat

is completely thawed, and continue to cook until the thermometer registers the degree of doneness you desire. This is the only accurate way to roast meat, whether it is cooked frozen or fresh.

Cooking time is certainly shortened if the meat is completely thawed or partially thawed, resulting of course in a saving of gas or electricity, a point in favor of this method of cooking frozen meat. In order to thaw meats, you must plan well in advance of your meal. A 5-pound roast will thaw completely in 24 hours at room temperature. In the food compartment of the refrigerator, it will need 36 to 48 hours. Defrost meats in their wrappers and cook them as soon as they are thawed, because all foods spoil rapidly after complete thawing.

Cooking partially thawed meats saves both thawing and cooking time. But here again, the use of a meat thermometer is necessary if you are going to have your meat cooked exactly the way you want it—rare, medium, or well done.

Steaks as well as roasts are superior in flavor and texture if they are broiled from the frozen state. The steaks will require an additional 20 to 30 minutes' broiling time, depending on the thickness.

Degrees for roasting meat

ROAST OF BEEF	INTERNAL TEMPERATURE
Rare	140° F.
Medium	160° F.
Well done	170° F.

ROAST OF LAMB	
Medium	175° F.
Well done	180° F.

VEAL AND PORK	
Well done	185° F.

Guide for cooking meat*

CUT OF MEAT	METHOD OF COOKING	DEGREE OF DONE- NESS	Approximate Minutes Per Pound	
			THAWED BEFORE COOKING	COOKED FROM THE FROZEN STATE
Standing rib roast	Roasting at 300° F.	Rare	18	43
		Medium	22	47
		Well done	30	55
Rolled-rib roast	Roasting at 300° F.	Rare	28	53
		Medium	32	56
		Well done	40	65
Pork-loin roast	Roasting at 300° F.	Well done		
Center cut			30 to 35	50 to 55
Rib or shoulder ends			50 to 55	70 to 75
Leg of lamb	Roasting at 300° F.	Well done	30 to 35	40 to 45
Beef rump	Braising	Well done	30 to 35	50
Porterhouse steak	Broiling	Rare to Medium		
1 inch thick			8 to 10	21 to 33
1½ inches thick			10 to 15	23 to 38
2 inches thick			20 to 30	33 to 43
Beef patties 1 inch thick	Pan-broiling	Medium	10 to 12	16 to 18

*From *Meat and Cookery,* Committee of the National Live Stock and Meat Board

CUT OF MEAT	METHOD OF COOKING	DEGREE OF DONE-NESS	Approximate Minutes Per Pound	
			THAWED BEFORE COOKING	COOKED FROM THE FROZEN STATE
Sausage patties	Pan-broiling	Well done	15 to 25	22 to 28
Lamb chops ¾ to 1½ inches thick	Pan-broiling	Well done	10 to 20	15 to 25
Pork chops ¾ inch thick	Braising	Well done	35 to 40	50 to 55

CHAPTER THREE

How to freeze poultry, game birds, and small game

Your home freezer can provide your table with a year-round supply of all kinds of poultry: chickens, turkeys, ducks, geese, guineas, quail, and pheasant. These great favorites may be preserved in any form—fryers, broilers, roasters, and so on. Frozen poultry is one of the most successful of all frozen foods, providing the birds are of high quality and well fed. Don't forget that freezing preserves the flavor and tenderness of poultry and game birds, but it cannot improve them or make tough fowl tender.

Freeze only the best. Grade A poultry are young, healthy, carefully raised birds. The feathers should be fully developed; the body well fleshed in the breast, thighs, drumsticks, and back. There should be few pinfeathers and a layer of fat under the skin. Ducks and geese should be broad-breasted, deep-fleshed, and moderately but not excessively fat.

When the season for broilers, fryers, and roasters rolls around, allot a reasonable space in your freezer for them. When they are plentiful is the time to buy, for then they are at their cheapest and best. Prepare them for the freezer exactly in the same manner as if you were going to broil, sauté, roast, or fricassee them that day. You can do this yourself, or your butcher will clean, truss, and split them, or cut them in any way you wish.

The way a chicken is to be cooked should be given some thought before you decide to buy or kill in quantity.

Broilers should be not over 12 weeks old and should weigh from 2 to 2½ pounds.

Fryers are about 20 weeks old and weigh from 3 to 3½ pounds.

Roasting chickens should not be over 1 year old and weigh from 4 to 5 pounds.

Fricassee chickens can be from 1 to 2 years old, reasonably fat, and weigh as much as 6 pounds.

Capons are from 8 to 10 months old, reasonably fat, and weigh from 7 to 10 pounds.

Baby turkeys are about 12 weeks old, weigh from 4 to 7 pounds, and may be split and broiled or stuffed and roasted.

Mature turkeys range in weight from 8 to 30 pounds and are at their prime for freezing from October through January.

Ducks are most plentiful in the spring. From 10 to 12 weeks old they are at their best and weigh from 5 to 6 pounds. Ducks are delicious braised with a favorite sauce as well as roasted, or steamed.

PREPARING POULTRY, GAME BIRDS, AND SMALL GAME FOR THE FREEZER

There are six steps in the preparation of poultry for the freezer. They are: killing, bleeding, plucking, chilling, dressing, and packaging. In most instances the first five of these steps have already been done for you before you buy the birds. Or you can have the birds prepared for you on order, as most locker plants will not only kill and dress poultry and cut them according to your specifications, but package them too, if you wish.

But for those who raise their own chickens, turkeys, and ducks, I am including information about the first five steps in preparing poultry for the freezer.

Killing and bleeding

For two weeks before the birds are to be killed, they should be restricted to an enclosed area where they are allowed access to all

THE DRUGSTORE FOLD is an easy way to make a close, tight wrap. Place the food in the center of the paper. Bring the ends of the paper above the meat and fold them over and over downward in a lock seal, drawing the paper as tightly to the food as possible, until the last fold rests firmly on the meat. Then fold the ends, fitting and pressing the paper close to the food to avoid air pockets.

Frigidaire

If Pliofilm, Saran, polyethylene, cellophane, or aluminum foil is used, a stockinette overwrap should be pulled snugly around the paper to prevent it from tearing. A label inserted under the stockinette makes identification easy.

Crosley

If steaks or chops are separated from each other by two layers of freezer paper, they may be easily separated for cooking while still in the frozen state, or a few may be cooked and the others returned to the freezer. Overwrap with moisture-vapor-proof paper and seal the edges with acetate tape.

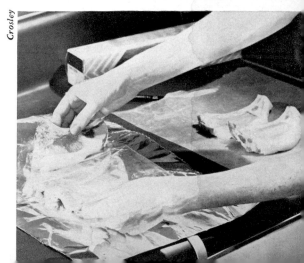

PACKAGING POULTRY. If poultry is carelessly wrapped and sealed so that the air can get in and the moisture out, it might as well never have been wrapped at all. **Above left:** Force out air pockets as you wrap moisture-vaporproof paper carefully around the bird. **Above right:** Fold the ends of the paper over, pressing out the air, and seal the edges with acetate tape. **Below left:** Cover the bird with stockinette to prevent any sharp bones from puncturing the paper and insert a label between the paper and the stockinette. **Below right:** Knot both ends of the stockinette tightly against the bird.

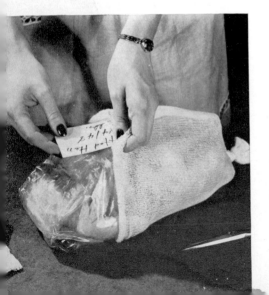 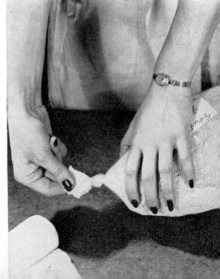

the food they want to consume. At this time, fish meal or fish oil should be eliminated from their diet and milk should be added to the daily rations. The fat is more evenly distributed through the flesh of milk-fed fowl than corn-fed birds.

The birds should be starved for 16 to 24 hours before they are killed, but plenty of fresh water should be available to help empty the crop and intestines. The fowl will then be much easier to clean, without any danger of the flavor of the flesh being spoiled.

Thorough bleeding is essential for fine-flavored meat and long storage life. Improperly bled birds have dark, reddened skin usually on the hips and wing tips, which detracts from their appearance. Congealed blood deteriorates rapidly and therefore lessens the storage time in the freezer for maximum flavor.

There are several satisfactory methods of killing birds to insure complete bleeding. A commonly used method of killing chickens and turkeys involves bleeding by severance of the jugular vein followed by braining, which involves piercing the medulla or back part of the brain through the mouth or eye. Braining, if correctly done, tends to loosen the feathers and facilitates plucking. It is not usually done to ducks and geese. Regardless of the method used to kill the birds, they should be hung to insure proper bleeding.

Hang the bird securely by the feet, head down. Grasp the head and cut through the jugular vein on the left side of the throat with a very sharp knife. Then, to brain, insert the knife blade in the cleft of the roof of the mouth, run it back in a line between the eye and ear, and give it a quarter turn.

Some people like to hang the bird in a suspended funnel to kill it, as the bird cannot struggle and there is no opportunity for it to break or bruise its wings.

Plucking

All kinds of poultry may be dry-plucked, although this is more difficult than scalding, especially with geese. If the bird is to be dry-plucked, the feathers must be removed immediately, for they will set again quickly. Keep the bird in the hanging position until it is thoroughly bled, but start plucking at once. Remove the tail feathers and large wing feathers first. Then proceed with the breast, sides, thighs, and legs. Finally, pick out the back feathers, the soft feathers on the neck, and the small feathers on the wings.

An easier method of plucking is to let the bird hang until it is thoroughly bled and then scald it. To scald, select a container large enough so that the bird can be completely covered with water with the exception of the feet. The temperature of the water should be from 130 to 145° F., but no hotter. Too hot water damages the tender skin of young birds, and the skin will tear as the feathers are removed. Plunge the bird in the hot water for 30 seconds, or until the wing and tail feathers pull out easily, moving it up and down to agitate the water and force the water through the feathers to the skin.

Once scalded, remove the wing and tail feathers first, then the leg feathers, and lastly the feathers on the body. Work quickly and rub the feathers off the body rather than pluck them. Start at the neck and work down. When all the feathers have been carefully removed, grasp the bird, neck in one hand, feet in the other, and turn it from side to side over a smokeless gas flame to singe off the hair feathers.

Ducks and geese are best scalded in water at a temperature just below the boiling point and just long enough to loosen the feathers. The ducks should be agitated vigorously during the scalding to force the water through the oily feathers to the skin. Geese may be scalded and then wrapped in a heavy sack or blanket for a few minutes to hold in the heat and to achieve an even scald. Trial will determine the correct temperature and the length of scalding time, as both over- or underscalding may result in the tearing out of small pieces of skin with the feathers during the plucking.

Plumping

After poultry has been plucked, the skin often has a loose appearance. If the bird is plunged for 7 to 10 seconds in water heated to 195° F., the slack will be taken up and the bird will have a nice plump appearance. Plunge the bird immediately into a bath of cold water for a couple of minutes after plumping.

Chilling

The quick removal of body heat is important once the bird is plucked and singed. This can be done before or after the bird is dressed or drawn. Chilling first hardens the fat and makes the poultry easier to draw. On the other hand, many authorities agree that the sooner the bird is eviscerated, the better will be the flavor of the flesh. Poultry may be chilled under refrigeration for 12 hours or overnight, or if no refrigeration is available, the body heat may be removed by placing the birds in ice water for 2 hours, or until they are completely chilled, replenishing the ice as it melts.

Dressing

Before a bird is drawn, the pinfeathers should be removed. This can be done quite neatly by using a strawberry huller, if you have one, or tweezers, otherwise catch the pinfeathers between thumb and a paring knife.

Scrub the skin in cold water with a brush or rough cloth and rinse the bird well. The bird is now ready to be drawn.

1. Cut off the feet. Grasp the leg and bend it back so that the skin is taut over the front leg joint. Cut across the front, bending back the leg to dislocate the joint, and cut across the back skin.
2. Cut out the oil sac in the tail.
3. Cut off the head.
4. Slit the neckskin down the center back to the shoulders and sever the neck at this point. Removing the neck makes it easier to remove the gullet, or esophagus, the crop, and the windpipe.
5. Loosen the crop, which is attached to the skin near the base of the neck, and the windpipe and esophagus, which are attached to the neckskin, by inserting the fingers into the neck opening and moving them around the cavity as far down as possible. Pull the crop, windpipe, and esophagus out as far as possible, cut them off at a point where they enter the body, and discard.

Birds may be drawn through either a vertical or horizontal incision.

6. (a) To draw a bird through a vertical incision, place the bird on its back and make an incision in the abdomen starting three inches above the vent. Continue the incision toward the tail and encircle the vent, cutting all around about three quarters of an inch from the center of the vent.

(b) To draw the bird through a horizontal incision, place the bird on its back and make a horizontal incision about 4 inches long just behind the breastbone. In this case a separate cut must be made around the vent in order to free the intestines so that the viscera can be removed.

7. Remove the viscera by inserting a forefinger into the opening and circle it around the intestines. Now hold the carcass firmly with one hand and insert the other hand through the opening and locate the gizzard near the center of the viscera. Grasp the gizzard firmly and draw the entrails completely out of the cavity.

8. Remove the lungs, making sure they are completely removed. This is important, as they contain blood. They are located in two sections, one on each side of the backbone over the ribs.

9. Make sure the heart is removed. It is found just under the wishbone.

10. Rinse out the cavity with cold water, or wipe it with a damp cloth, and drain thoroughly.

11. Detach the heart, liver, and gizzard from the other entrails.

12. Discard the heart sac, cut off the blood vessels, and wash the heart to remove the blood.

13. Cut out the gall sac from the liver, being very careful not to break it, and discard any part of the liver that might be stained green by contact with the gall bladder. Should the bladder break, you will not only have to discard the liver but any part of the chicken that it might have touched.

14. Make a slit in one side of the gizzard, being careful not to cut the inner sac. Force the slit open with the thumbs and pull the gizzard gently but firmly away from the sac. Discard the sac with the intestines and remaining viscera.

15. Wash the giblets in cold water and drain them well.

DRESSING BROILERS

Broilers are dressed by splitting the birds up the back.

1. Cut off the head and legs of young chicken not over twelve weeks old.

2. Slit the skin from shoulder to tail along the right side of the backbone.

3. With heavy kitchen shears, cut along this line from the tail to the shoulders. With a sharp knife, cut from the tip of the tail up to and encircling the vent three quarters of an inch from the center of the vent.

4. Spread the bird open at the back, lay it flat on the table flesh down, and remove the viscera, lungs, and kidneys.

5. Rinse the cavity of the bird with cold water, or wipe it with a damp cloth.

6. Prepare the giblets (see Dressing).

Broilers may be left split, still joined at the breastbone, or they may be separated into halves or quarters. The backbone may be completely removed before the broilers are packaged for the freezer.

DRESSING FRYING CHICKENS

Chickens weighing about 3 to 3⅓ pounds are perfect for deep-fat frying or for sautéeing. They may be drawn, or dressed, at the same time they are cut into serving portions. Use a very sharp knife.

1. Cut off the wings at the joints and either remove the wing tips to use in making soup stock or slip the tip of each wing under the second joint to fasten it securely in place.

2. Remove the legs, pulling each leg in turn away from the body of the bird so the skin is taut. Sever the skin and flesh down to the thigh joint and free the leg at the hip. Separate the drumstick from the thigh.

3. Separate the back from the breast by cutting from one wing joint to the other, encircling the bird around the vent.

4. Place the bird on the table. Grasp the vent end with one hand and the top of the breastbone with the other and gently pull the breast end up. The breast will snap away from the wing joints and it may be cut into two parts, or if the breast section is quite large, smaller pieces may be cut, as desired.

5. Grasp the vent end of the back with one hand; slip the forefinger of the other hand under the entrails and lift them out.

6. Remove the lungs from the backbone of the chicken, and wash the back with cold water or wipe it with a damp cloth.

7. Prepare the giblets (see Dressing).

The back may be halved, but there is so little meat on it that it does not pay to take up freezer space with this part of the bird, or the neck. Make concentrated soup stock instead, and freeze the stock.

What have you got from one fryer? Two wings, two thighs, two drumsticks, two pieces of breast meat, and the giblets.

DRESSING FRICASSEE AND STEWING CHICKENS

Large chickens for braising, poaching, or stewing should be cut up the same as fryers to conserve freezer space.

DRESSING GAME BIRDS

Wild fowl of all kinds—pheasant, grouse, quail, wild geese, wild ducks, and guinea hens—are prepared in the same manner as domestic fowl. They should be properly bled right after they are bagged, and a wise hunter will also chill the birds instead of stuffing them into a hunting bag.

Pluck game birds in the same manner as other poultry, rather than skin them. Skinning causes loss of flavor and drying of the flesh. The birds should be scalded and plucked as soon after killing as possible. Remove as much of the shot as possible and roll them in melted paraffin to remove the pinfeathers and down.

Game birds should be drawn as soon as possible after they have been shot. If there is no time to do the complete job, remove the craw and intestines so that the flavor of the meat will not be spoiled by the partly digested food. This applies especially to wild ducks, which might have been feeding on strongly flavored water plants and fish. In any event, clean them thoroughly as soon as possible, for the flesh of game birds deteriorates rapidly, particularly in the wounded areas.

All game birds should hang at a temperature just above freezing for at least 48 hours before they are packaged for the freezer.

Game birds may be prepared for roasting or cut up for sautéeing, depending on how you wish to use them.

DRESSING SMALL GAME ANIMALS

Rabbits, squirrels, and other small game animals should be dressed as soon as possible after they are shot. Immediately after killing them, behead them, bleed them thoroughly, and hang them in an airy place at a temperature a little above freezing for 48 hours. Then skin and dress them. Wipe them with a cloth dipped in scalding water and cut them into serving pieces, as with frying chickens. Sometimes, to save freezer space, only the thick back and hindquarters, known as "the saddle," are frozen. Use the rest, while fresh, for stews or casseroles.

How to bone a bird

Squab, chickens, capons, and turkeys may all be boned before they are frozen to conserve freezer space. The boned poultry may be stuffed and rolled, or made into galantines or ballotines before they are frozen, ready for the most important occasion. The entrails are removed as the bird is boned.

Remove the head and the feet. Cut off all but the first joint of the wings and the neck, but keep the skin of the neck as long as possible. With a very sharp pointed knife, or a boning knife, cut a straight line down the back from neck to tail. Cut off the tail.

Now begin to scrape and cut the flesh from the backbone down to the shoulder blade, being careful not to pierce the skin. When

you come to the leg and wing joints, cut through the joints. Proceed
in the same manner on the other side and the meat will be free from
the carcass and the entire carcass with the entrails may be lifted out,
leaving the fleshy part of the bird and the skin intact. Scrape the
flesh from the thigh bone, cut through the leg joint, and pull out the
thigh bone. Continue to scrape the flesh from the leg and wing
bones and draw the bones out of the flesh.

PACKAGING POULTRY

Effective packaging of poultry is necessary to keep the flesh from
drying out, to prevent freezer burn, and to keep the meat from being
contaminated with other flavors. Without proper moisture-vaporproof wrappings, dehydration is bound to take place at the low storage temperature and the birds will be tough and dry when they are
cooked.

Poultry should be packaged according to the type of bird, the
method by which it is going to be cooked, and the number of servings for a meal.

To estimate the number of servings, weigh the bird after it has
been killed, bled, and plucked. Allow 1 pound per serving of
chickens, guineas, and capons, from ¾ to 1 pound for turkeys, and
1½ pounds for geese and ducks. This additional allowance for
geese and ducks is necessary because the carcasses are bigger and
there is more loss in weight when these birds are dressed and
cooked.

Birds for roasting are best at a certain age:

Chickens	5 to 9 months
Capons	7 to 10 months
Turkeys	5 to 9 months
Guineas	5 to 10 months
Geese	5 to 11 months
Ducks	4 to 6 months

Cut-up poultry takes less freezer space than whole birds and if
freezer space is limited, it is wise to freeze only the choice pieces of

meat, such as the breast and thighs. The backbones, wing tips, necks, and legs can be made into concentrated soup stock, and the stock frozen, or the cooked meat from the wings and drumsticks may be made into croquettes or creamed and the prepared dishes frozen.

Whole poultry

Once the bird is dressed it should be wrapped and frozen at once. If this is not possible, wrap the bird and place it in the refrigerator until it can be put in the freezer, but in any event no more than 1 hour should elapse from wrapping to freezing.

Wrap the giblets in moisture-vaporproof paper and place them in the cavity of the bird, tuck them under the wing, or freeze them in a separate package.

Trussing before freezing makes the carcass more compact, saves storage space, and glorifies the appearance of the cooked bird. Trussed birds are all ready to put in the oven or on the spit the moment they are taken from the freezer.

Fold the neckskin down over the back. Bend the wings around and lock them in back by twisting the wing tips over the forewings. Tie the center of a long piece of string around the leg joints, push the legs down, and tie them securely to the tail. Bring the ends of the string up the back of the bird, hitch them around the wings, and tie them over the neckskin in back.

Moisture-vaporproof Saran wrap, aluminum foil, laminated papers, Pliofilm, and Polyethylene are all excellent protectors. Wrap the bird carefully, forcing out any air pockets which might form during the wrapping. Fasten the paper with an acetate sealing tape, slip a stockinette over the bird if the wrapping needs this extra protection, and knot the ends close to the body of the bird. Slip a label between the paper and the stockinette for future identification.

Stuffed whole poultry

Frozen poultry, stuffed and ready for the oven, is a great convenience at any time of the year when entertaining is expected to be heavy, but is especially useful for Thanksgiving, Christmas, and New Year's festivities. Fill the bird cavity loosely with dry bread crumbs, mixed with a little chopped celery and onion sautéed in butter and modestly seasoned with salt and pepper and thyme, sage, or savory. Do not overseason and *do not use pork-sausage meat, oysters, or nuts in the dressing.*

Stuffed poultry should not be stored longer than 3 months in the home freezer. Freeze birds only for the sake of convenience, for special occasions, not for long storage.

Wrap stuffed birds in the same manner as whole poultry. No overwrap is needed if a laminated paper is used, but aluminum foil or transparent papers such as Pliofilm, Polyethylene, and Saran have greater flexibility and can be smoothed to conform to the shape of the bird, eliminating air pockets. All these wrapping papers should be protected by a stockinette overwrap.

Broilers

Turkeys, as well as chickens and guineas, halved or quartered and ready for broiling, make valuable additions to the food supply in your freezer. It isn't necessary to wait for a special event in order to enjoy the flavor of turkey. Turkey is frequently an excellent buy in the non-holiday season. A portion of turkey to suit your family requirements may often take the place of a Sunday roast.

Wrap and freeze the giblets separately. Place two pieces of freezer paper between the two halves of chickens or other small birds so that they can be separated while still frozen. Then wrap the two halves securely in a moisture-vaporproof bag or paper. If you wish to package more than one broiler together, depending on the number of servings needed at one time, the halves may be nested with a double thickness of the paper between them. If the leg ends are sharp, wrap them so that they will not puncture the outer wrapping. Turkey halves may be packaged separately for broiling or roasting. Envelop them compactly in moisture-vapor-proof paper, excluding as much air as possible.

Cut poultry

Tender chickens, for frying or sautéeing; well-fattened birds past their prime for roasting, but suitable for braising or stewing; ducks and geese, and larger birds such as turkeys, can all be cut into serving pieces before they are frozen as an effective method of conserving space. Wrap each piece in a fold of freezer paper and pack tightly into a moisture-proof carton that can be heat-sealed. Use small-, medium-, or large-sized packages to suit your family needs. If you are freezing a large quantity of disjointed fowl, you might lay aside and package certain choice pieces for special recipes.

PACKAGING GAME BIRDS AND SMALL GAME ANIMALS

Game birds, rabbits, and squirrels are packaged in the same manner as poultry. Some States do not permit game to be stored for more than 10 days, so it is wise to consult your State Conservation Department, or your local game warden, for details.

Label and freeze

Label each package of poultry or game intelligently with the kind, the method of preparation, the weight, the number of servings, the date frozen, and any other pertinent information that will be of help to you weeks or months later, when many of the things you think you will have remembered have been forgotten.

HOW TO COOK FROZEN POULTRY

Poultry may be cooked from the frozen state with excellent results. It requires longer cooking and should be cooked at moderate temperatures in order to let the heat penetrate and cook the bird uniformly. However, the quality of poultry is not affected if it is thawed, providing it is cooked soon after thawing. If you wish to stuff a bird that has been frozen unstuffed, it is necessary to thaw it completely before the stuffing can go in.

Thaw frozen poultry in the unopened package either in the refrigerator or at room temperature. A 3-pound bird will thaw in about 6 hours in the refrigerator and in about 3 hours at room temperature. A capon will thaw in about 24 hours in the refrigerator, or 12 hours at room temperature. A turkey needs 48 hours in the refrigerator, or 24 hours at room temperature, to defrost completely.

Roasting

Rub the inside of the bird with salt and pepper. Fill the cavity, if desired, with your favorite stuffing. Do not pack it tightly, as the filling must have room to expand. As it expands it absorbs some of the juices as they cook out of the meat and for this reason any bird is juicier and the flesh is more flavorful and succulent if the bird is not stuffed. Rather, put in the cavity a few sprigs of parsley, a small stalk of celery, and an onion, quartered, or a few shallots. Some like a clove of garlic or a spray of tarragon or thyme. Bake the dressing separately, so that it will not rob the flesh of its moisture and flavor.

Close the cavity with skewers, or sew it up with kitchen thread, and truss the wings and legs close to the body. Rub the skin with butter and sprinkle it with salt and pepper. Place the bird on a rack in a shallow roasting pan, breast down, for half the cooking period, to keep the breast meat moist, then turn it for the rest of the roasting time to brown the breast. Baste occasionally with the pan drippings to keep the skin moist. For a rich, brown color, add 1 teaspoon tomato paste to the drippings in the pan ½ hour before the bird is done and baste frequently. To test for doneness, insert the prongs of a fork in the thigh. If the juice that runs out is clear and has no pink tinge, the bird is done.

TO ROAST HALF A TURKEY

Half a turkey is generally a better size for the average family and may be roasted beautifully. Season the cavity with salt and pepper and place the turkey, cut side down, in the roasting pan. If dressing is desired, mound about 4 cups of seasoned bread crumbs on the bottom of the roaster and place the bird over the crumbs. Brush the skin with melted butter and roast the turkey in a slow oven (325° F.), basting occasionally, until it tests done. A 6-pound half turkey, thawed, will require about 2½ hours roasting time. Allow an extra half hour if roasted from the frozen state.

TIME TABLE FOR ROASTING THAWED POULTRY

BIRD	POUNDS DRESSED WEIGHT	DEGREES F. OVEN TEMP.	APPROXIMATE HOURS ROASTING
Chicken	4 to 5	350	1½ to 2
Duck	5 to 6	350	2 to 2½
Goose	10 to 12	325	3 to 4
Guinea	2 to 2½	350	1½
Turkey	6 to 9	350	2 to 2½
	10 to 13	325	2½ to 3½
	14 to 17	300	4 to 5
	18 to 25	275	5½ to 7

TO ROAST UNTHAWED BIRDS

Allow 30 minutes longer cooking time for a 4- to 5-pound chicken or duck, 1 hour longer for a 6- to 8-pound capon or turkey, 1½ hours longer for a 10-pound goose or turkey, and 2 hours longer for a very large bird.

Broiling

Thaw broilers in the refrigerator overnight.

Brush thawed split broilers with melted butter and sprinkle them with salt and pepper. Place them on a preheated oiled broiler rack skin side down and broil 5 inches from the flame. Turn the birds frequently and brush them with melted butter each time they are turned. Broil for 25 to 50 minutes, depending on the thickness and tenderness of the meat, or until the skin side is golden and the juice

that runs from the thigh when it is pricked with a fork has no tinge
of pink. A little finely chopped fresh herb, such as tarragon, thyme,
parsley, chervil, or chives, heated with the basting butter will add a
subtle flavor.

Broilers may be broiled without preliminary thawing in exactly
the same manner as the thawed halves. Allow half again as much
broiling time.

Frying

Poultry that is to be fried in hot deep fat should be thawed completely, or the outside will be brown and crisp while the center is
still cold. Some like to steam the pieces first until tender, especially
if the bird is not so young as it should be for frying. When thawed,
wipe the pieces dry and dip them in a batter made by beating 1 egg
lightly and stirring in ¾ cup milk, 1 cup flour, and ½ teaspoon
salt. Fry the pieces a few at a time in deep fat (350° F.) for 15 to
20 minutes, depending on the size and age of the bird and whether
or not the pieces were presteamed. Drain on absorbent paper and
sprinkle with salt and pepper.

Sautéeing

Poultry may be sautéed or pan-fried directly from the frozen
state, or partially or completely thawed. Dredge the pieces in flour
and brown them on all sides in hot butter. When brown, reduce the
flame, cover the skillet tightly, and sauté for about 30 minutes, or
until done. A little wine or stock, a clove of garlic, chopped parsley,
some finely chopped onion or shallots, a few tomatoes, peeled and
quartered, a leaf of sweet basil—any or all may be added for in-
finite variations. Allow half as much cooking time for the thawed
chicken as the frozen.

Fricasseeing

Older birds need long, slow cooking in liquid or steam to tender-
ize them. Cut-up chicken or other poultry may be removed from

the freezer, dredged with seasoned flour, and browned slowly in hot butter without any preliminary thawing. The browned pieces of poultry are then transferred to a casserole. Enough water or stock is added barely to cover them, the casserole is covered tightly, and the bird is baked in a moderate oven (350° F.) for 2 to 3 hours, or until the pieces are tender. Vegetables may be added when the bird is partially cooked. Tomato juice or wine may be substituted for part of the water or stock.

Stewing

Stewing differs from fricasseeing in that the pieces are not browned, but are cooked in seasoned liquid for 2 to 3 hours, or until tender.

CHAPTER FOUR

How to freeze fish and sea food

The ardent fisherman need no longer be forced to give away most of his proud catch to his friends. If he owns a home freezer he can enjoy the flavor of freshly caught fish long after his outing, by storing them at zero temperature.

As soon as the fish is landed it should be killed and either iced or refrigerated until it can be prepared for the freezer. Speed is essential, for fish is an extremely perishable food. It deteriorates rapidly from the moment it leaves the water and within a few hours bacteria from air and water begin their work of contamination. Packing fish in ice or refrigerating them merely retards the bacterial action, as the particular organisms which attack fish can survive at lower temperatures than those which attack meat.

The storage period for fish is relatively brief. One to 3 months is the maximum, and the more fatty a fish, the shorter the storage period. Fatty fish such as salmon, mackerel, and herring should not be stored more than 6 weeks. Fortunately there are more varieties of lean than fatty fish, and these retain their quality and flavor for as long as 3 months.

Some sections of the country have limits on the length of time fish can be stored, so consult your local game warden before packaging fish for your freezer.

Fatty fish include, among others: Barracuda, bonito, butterfish,

eels, herring, kingfish, mackerel, millet, pilchard, pompano, rock-
fish, rosefish, salmon, shad, squid, catfish, tuna, whitefish

Lean fish include, among others: Bass, blowfish, blue runner,
bluefish, burbot, swordfish, cod, crevalle, croaker, flounder, fluke,
gar, grouper, grunt, haddock, halibut, lingcod, muskellunge, perch,
pickerel, pike, pollock, porgy, red drum, red snapper, scrod, sea
trout, sheepshead, smelt, snook, sunfish, sole, spot, trout, weakfish,
whiting, wolffish

PREPARING FRESHLY CAUGHT FISH FOR THE FREEZER

Fish should be prepared for the freezer as soon as reasonably
possible and in exactly the same way as if they were going to be
cooked immediately. Small fish may be left whole and pan-dressed
—scales, entrails, and fins removed. The backbone may also be cut
out and, to save freezer space, the head and tail are usually discarded. Large fish are generally fileted, or are cut crosswise into
steaks an inch or more thick.

It is not an unpleasant task to clean and dress a fish. It can be
done easily and quickly with no more equipment than a sharp,
strong knife. If you anticipate a busy fishing season, a fish scaler is
helpful, but not essential.

To clean and pan-dress a whole fish

1. Wash the fish quickly in cold salted water, using 1 tablespoon
salt to each quart of water.
2. Place the fish on several thicknesses of strong paper and grasp
the head firmly. Scrape the scales off from tail to head with a sharp
knife held at an almost vertical angle.
3. "Run" the dorsal and pelvic fins. This means cut down into
the flesh on either side of the fins, then pull them out. Never cut off
the fins with scissors.
4. Slit the entire length of the belly from head to vent and remove the entrails.
5. Cut off the head, including the pectoral fins, and the tail.

6. Dip the fish quickly in cold salted water and remove the clotted blood and any remaining membranes.

To bone a fish such as a pike or bass

Insert a very sharp knife with a pointed blade into the flesh on one side of the backbone and cut from head to tail close to the bone. Turn the fish over and cut from head to tail on the other side. Lift out the entire backbone of the fish and pull out any small bones that remain.

To filet a flat fish such as a flounder or pompano

1. Cut through the flesh along the back of the fish on one side of the dorsal fin from tail to head.
2. Cut across the fish just behind the head down to the backbone.
3. Turn the knife flat and cut off the flesh from the backbone from head to tail. The knife runs along the rib bones and the filet is cut off in one piece.
4. Turn the fish and repeat the process on the other side.

TO SKIN THE FILETS

Loosen the skin at the broad end of the filet. Hold the flesh firmly against the table or a board, grasp the skin firmly, and strip it off.

Or, place the filet skin side down. Cut through the flesh to the skin ½ inch from the tail end. Hold the free end of the skin firmly against the table. Flatten the knife on the skin and pull the knife forward, cutting the flesh from the skin.

TO REMOVE FISHY ODOR FROM HANDS AND UTENSILS, rub the fish knife and your hands well with moistened salt, rinse off the salt with hot water, then wash thoroughly with soap or detergent.

PACKAGING FISH FOR THE FREEZER

Before packaging lean fish—whole, steaks, or filets—should be dipped for 20 seconds in cold salted water, made by dissolving 1 cup salt in 1 gallon ice water. Fatty fish should not be treated with a salt solution.

Whole fish

Wrap whole fish individually in moisture-vaporproof paper. If whole fish are small, several or enough for one meal may be packaged together, individually wrapped, in a top-opening carton or bag. Seal and label.

Whole fish may be stuffed with a favorite forcemeat before it is frozen, but the time of storage for even a lean fish should then be limited to 1 month.

TO GLAZE A WHOLE FISH

Whole fish has a tendency to dry out in frozen storage. An excellent way to prevent this is to place the fish on a tray and put it in the freezer until it is frozen. Then dip the fish in ice water several times, chilling it between dips. The water will freeze on the fish almost immediately and a layer of ice ¼ inch thick can be quickly built up to encase the fish in a glacial shroud. Wrap the ice-encrusted fish in moisture-vaporproof paper, seal the edges with acetate tape, label, and store in the freezer.

Filets and steaks

Pack filets and steaks in layers in top-opening cartons with two sheets of freezer paper between layers so they will separate easily when taken from the freezer. Close the carton, label, overwrap with moisture-vaporproof paper, and heat-seal all open edges with a warm hand iron, or seal with acetate tape.

Fish soups

Use the fish heads, bones, and leftover scraps of flesh to make a good chowder or fish stew or a concentrated fish stock. Pour the soup, stew, or stock into leakproof cartons or glass jars, leaving 1 inch headspace, seal, and freeze.

HOW TO COOK FROZEN FISH

Frozen fish is cooked just like fresh fish. It is best when cooked directly from the frozen state, but extra cooking time must be allowed. It may, however, be partially or completely thawed, depending on which method is more convenient.

To thaw, place the unopened package on the shelf in the refrigerator to defrost. A 1-pound package of frozen fish will thaw in 8 to 10 hours in the refrigerator. The same quantity will thaw in about 3 hours at room temperature, but there is less loss of juices and flavors if the fish is thawed slowly. Once thawed, cook it promptly, while it is still cold.

It is very difficult to give absolutely accurate cooking times for fish, since so much depends on the thickness, freshness, and texture of the particular fish. But the surest way is to cook the fish until the flesh flakes easily when tested with a toothpick, or the prongs of a fork. Just be careful not to dry it out by overcooking.

Broiling

Broiling is one of the simplest methods of cooking whole fish, filets, or steaks. Whole split fish and filets should be broiled on one side only and not turned, since the turning is apt to break the fish into pieces.

Don't use a broiler rack. Rather, use a shallow, flat pan. Heat both the broiler and the pan to 450° F. Oil the hot pan generously with olive oil and place the fish on it, skin side down. Dot the surface of the fish with butter and broil the fish 4 or 5 inches from the flame, basting it several times with butter, until it is golden brown and the flesh flakes easily.

Whole fish and fish steaks need broiling on both sides and should be basted frequently with butter, or a mixture of melted butter and white wine. They should be turned ever so carefully with two large spatulas. But a small word of warning: broiling is not a suitable method of cooking large whole fish. Fish that are thick through the center should be split and broiled open with frequent bastings of butter, or cooked in another manner—perhaps baked or poached.

Serve broiled fish simply, with a wedge of lemon, or with melted butter mixed with plenty of chopped parsley and lemon juice.

BROILING TIME

In general, small whole fish, such as weakfish, sea bass, or flounder, require 3 to 8 minutes' broiling on each side. Fish steaks 1 inch thick will take 4 or 5 minutes' broiling on each side. Whole fish, split, take from 8 to 14 minutes. Filets need from 5 to 8 minutes. If fish is broiled from the frozen state, the broiling time must be doubled.

Baking

Baking is the best method of cooking large fish, although small whole fish, fish filets, and steaks may be cooked quickly and deliciously in a hot oven. The fish should not be turned, even a large one, as the heat of the oven will cook it evenly from both the top and the bottom.

Preheat the oven to 450° F. Oil the baking pan, or line it with lettuce leaves, to prevent the fish from sticking. Place the fish in the pan and butter the surface generously. Bake the fish, basting frequently with butter, or a mixture of melted butter and white or red wine, until the fish is delicately brown and the flesh flakes easily.

Baked fish may be served with parsley-butter or lemon-butter sauce, with tomato sauce, cream sauce, egg sauce, wine sauce, or hollandaise.

Fish ranging from 4 to 8 pounds are excellent when stuffed and baked. If the fish was frozen unstuffed, it must be thawed before it can be stuffed and skewered. A favorite bread stuffing may be used. A vegetable stuffing of thinly sliced onions, shallots, or scallions, sliced tomatoes, and chopped parsley gives flavor to fish without robbing it of its natural juices. Season the stuffing with salt and pepper and add plenty of butter. The fish may be basted with tomato juice, or with fresh or sour cream.

BAKING TIME

Allow approximately 12 minutes per pound for baking thawed fish. If baking fish directly from the frozen state, about 20 minutes per pound should be allowed.

Sautéeing or pan-frying

Sautéeing is one of the best ways to cook small fish or fish filets, and plenty of butter or fat is needed to keep the fish from drying out over the brisk heat. Sauté the fish until it is golden brown on both sides and just until the flesh flakes easily. Be careful not to overcook it. Fish does not need tenderizing by long cooking; quite to the contrary, overcooking is apt to make it tough.

The fish may be dipped in egg yolk beaten with a little milk and rolled in flour or bread crumbs. When cooked, sprinkle the fish with salt and pepper and serve with a wedge of lemon and several sprays of water cress.

Sauté Meunière is a favorite way to serve sautéed fish. When cooked, remove the fish to a hot platter and sprinkle it with salt, pepper, and lemon juice. Add butter and plenty of chopped parsley to the pan, cook until the butter begins to foam, and pour over the fish. Garnish with lemon slices.

Sauté Amandine is another favorite. Sauté the fish in butter until it is golden and the flesh flakes easily. Remove to a hot serving platter and sprinkle with salt, pepper, and lemon juice. Add more butter to the pan and some shredded blanched almonds. Cook, stirring, until the almonds are golden and pour almonds and butter over the fish.

SAUTÉEING TIME

Sauté thawed small fish or fish filets for 3 to 5 minutes on one side, turn, and continue to sauté on the other side for another 3 minutes. The time must be doubled for frozen small fish or filets.

Frying

Dip small fish or filets in flour, then in beaten egg, and roll them in bread crumbs or corn meal. Fry a few at a time in hot deep fat (380° F.) for 3 to 5 minutes, or until golden brown, and drain on absorbent paper. Sprinkle the fish with salt and pepper and serve with tomato sauce, *sauce diable,* or tartar sauce. The fish should be thawed before they are fried.

Poaching

Any fish, whether it is whole or cut into filets, is at its most succulent when it is poached in *court-bouillon,* or cooked in seasoned water just below the boiling point. It is the ideal way for salmon, whether you plan to serve it hot or cold. The *court-bouillon* may be strained and used as the base of a lovely wine sauce, or gelatin may be added, the broth chilled and used for fish aspic.

To make a *court-bouillon* you need fish stock, which you may have frugally concentrated from the head, bones, and trimmings of fish, and then frozen, or else you must buy the bones and trimmings from your fish dealer and simmer them in 2 quarts of water for about 20 minutes to extract the flavor.

At any rate, into your fish poacher, or any kettle that is large and long enough to hold your fish, put about 2 quarts of good stock, or enough to cover the fish, and add 1 cup wine, red or white, 1 onion stuck with 2 cloves, 4 peppercorns, ½ bay leaf, 4 sprigs of parsley, a pinch of thyme, and salt to taste. Bring the stock to a boil and simmer for 10 minutes.

Tie the fish in cheesecloth and tie the ends into loops so it will be easy to lift the fish from the pan when it is cooked. Lower it gently into the liquid and poach the fish until the flesh flakes easily. Be careful not to overcook, and do not let the liquid boil. Lift the fish from the kettle, unwrap, and roll it onto a warm serving platter. Remove the skin carefully and serve the fish hot with a hot lemon-butter-parsley sauce, or with any favorite fish sauce. Or chill the fish and serve it simply with mayonnaise, the platter beautifully garnished with water cress, sliced tomatoes, and cucumbers. Or coat it with mayonnaise *chaud-froid,* glaze it with aspic, and serve mayonnaise on the side. The fish may be elaborately embellished with little cut-outs of black olive or truffles.

Fish filets may be poached in *court-bouillon* either flat or fashioned into small rolls and tied securely. The rolls may be stuffed with a fish forcemeat. Once the fish is cooked and removed to a serving dish, the *court-bouillon* may be thickened with egg yolks, or with flour rubbed to a paste with butter, to make the sauce. Finish the sauce with heavy cream, pour it over the filets, and sprinkle with parsley.

POACHING TIME

Large fish need from 6 to 10 minutes per pound poaching time, and filets require about 1 minute per ounce. Double the poaching time if the fish is poached from the frozen state.

HOW TO FREEZE LOBSTERS

Select only live lobsters. Small lobsters, 2 pounds or less, are the most delicate. Larger ones are apt to be tough. Plunge them into boiling salted water or *court-bouillon* (see Index) and simmer them from 10 to 20 minutes, depending on their size. Cool and split. Discard the intestinal vein and the sac behind the head and put two halves together again to form a whole lobster. Wrap in Saran, Pliofilm, or aluminum foil, overwrap, and freeze to serve cold, when thawed, with mayonnaise or rémoulade or ravigote sauce. Or remove the meat from the tail and claws, pack the meat in Cellophane-lined cartons, leaving ½ inch headspace, and freeze for use in lobster Newburg, or other cooked lobster dishes.

HOW TO FREEZE SHRIMP

Shrimp may be frozen cooked or uncooked. The uncooked retain their quality better, while the cooked are easier to use. All you have to do with the cooked frozen shrimp for use in cocktails and salads is to let them thaw.

Wash uncooked shrimp thoroughly in cold water. Remove the shells and the intestinal veins that run down the backs. Rinse and drain. Package in cartons with two layers of freezer paper between layers of shrimp. Wrap the carton in moisture-vaporproof paper, seal, and freeze.

To freeze cooked shrimp, simmer the shrimp in boiling salted water or *court-bouillon* (see Index) for 10 minutes. Cool them in the cooking liquor, shell them, and devein. Pack the cooked shrimp in cartons, leaving ½ inch headspace. Overwrap, seal, and freeze promptly. Do not plan to store for more than 1 month. Freeze cooked shrimp only for convenience, as they tend to toughen during long storage at zero temperature.

CRABS

During the warmer months from May to October, crabs shed the hard shells that begin to pinch a little as the crustaceans grow one size larger. For 2 to 3 days the hard-shelled crab is a soft-shelled crab and if caught at this particular time in its life, it is entirely tender and edible, including the new embryo shell.

Soft-shelled crabs

Cut off the head, about ¼ inch behind the eyes. Squeeze gently to force out the green bubble behind the eyes which contains a bitter fluid. Lift the soft shell where it comes to a point at each side and cut off the white gills with kitchen scissors. Peel back the apron and cut it off. Dip the crabs in cold salted water and package them in cartons with two layers of freezer paper between layers of crab. Overwrap the carton with moisture-vaporproof paper, seal, and freeze.

Soft-shelled crabs may be partially thawed for 15 minutes in lightly salted milk and broiled under a moderate flame for about 15 minutes on one side and 10 on the other, basting them frequently

with melted butter. Serve them sprinkled with lemon juice and parsley. Or they may be sautéed in butter directly from the frozen state
for about 10 minutes on one side and 6 on the other, and served
with lemon-butter sauce, with shredded almonds browned in butter,
with finely chopped mixed herbs such as tarragon, chives, and parsley wilted in butter, or with *sauce diable*.

Hard-shelled crabs

Wash hard-shelled crabs in cold water. Drop them into boiling
water containing 1 teaspoon salt for every quart of water and simmer them for 15 minutes. Drain and cool thoroughly. Remove the
edible meat from the body and claws and pack it into moisture-
vaporproof cartons, leaving ½ inch headspace. Seal and freeze.

Defrost the crab meat and serve it very cold as salad or cocktail
with mayonnaise, or a more highly seasoned sauce such as rémoulade, ravigote, or Russian dressing.

HOW TO FREEZE OYSTERS AND CLAMS

Oysters and clams must be handled very rapidly and carefully.
Wash the shells in cold running water to remove any external sand.
Shuck the bivalves, saving the liquor, and discarding any dead or
injured ones. Wash them in a brine made of 2 tablespoons salt dissolved in a quart of cold water, and drain. Package the oysters or
clams in liquid-tight containers and fill the containers to within ½
inch of the top with the liquor. Seal and freeze quickly.

Oysters and clams may be thawed and served cold with a cocktail sauce, or may be used in soups and chowders, or baked sea-
food casseroles.

CHAPTER FIVE

Vegetables—how to freeze, and new ways to cook them

TO FREEZE OR NOT TO FREEZE

Vegetables that you enjoy raw and crisp, such as salad greens, radishes, celery, tomatoes, cucumbers, and onions, do not freeze satisfactorily.

Most of the rest that are normally cooked before they are served freeze well and retain much of their nutritive value, color, flavor, and fresh goodness if the rules for freezing them are strictly followed. But, like any processed food, frozen vegetables are never quite as good, nor should you expect them to be, as garden vegetables cooked in a small amount of water until barely tender and served, bathed in sweet butter, in a matter of minutes from the time they were picked from the vine or plucked from the earth.

Many vegetables are available every month of the year, so there is little reason to freeze them. When root cellars and cold-storage warehouses are exhausted, a new crop begins to arrive in Northern markets from the Carolinas, Texas, Florida, and California. Our Southern States keep our markets supplied with a large variety of vegetables the year round, which can be easily prepared and quickly cooked to grace our daily meals.

As a matter of honest fact, I can think of only two reasons why anyone should monopolize valuable freezer space with quantities of home-frozen vegetables:

1. If you and your family are inordinately fond of a vegetable such as zucchini that is in season for only a short period during the year and which is not frozen by commercial freezing companies.
2. If you have a surplus of choice vegetables from your own farm or garden that would go to waste if you did not freeze them.

And I do mean CHOICE, for you get out of your freezer only the quality that you put in. The finest, tenderest, most flavorful vegetables are the ones to freeze. Immature vegetables have not developed their maximum flavor and overripe ones have lost flavor, are tough or mushy, and do not keep well in the frozen state.

And I do mean SURPLUS. Your family table should not be sacrificed on the altar of home freezing. Gather and eat those tiny, sweet green peas, those tender stalks of asparagus every day direct from the garden while they are in season—twice a day if possible. Don't freeze the best from your garden and serve the overgrown or inferior vegetables at your table. Remember that not until twelve months roll by will you again enjoy that particular vegetable at its supreme height of flavor and succulence. If, after eating all the fresh, choice vegetables from your garden that you can eat, you still have some left—those are the ones to freeze.

If you don't have a surplus of choice vegetables from your farm or garden, if you can't arrange with a local farmer to supply you with your favorite vegetables freshly harvested, it is wiser by far to depend on the commercially frozen products to supply your daily needs. Commercial plants can do a better job with vegetables than you can and, generally, at a lower price if you take into consideration your time.

Commercial freezing companies contract with farmers to grow the varieties of vegetables best suited to freezing. They buy in vast quantities, therefore cheaply. They process faster because of ultramodern assembly lines and highly mechanized preparation. They have machines that sort or cut the vegetables into matched sizes or pieces. The scalding is uniform and exact. The packaging is thorough and efficient. From the earth to the freezer, every step along the way is supervised by laboratory technicians and chemists. Keep in your freezer at all times several packages of your favorite vegetables that have been commercially, scientifically frozen by a reliable company.

That sounds as if I were being recompensed by commercial packers to hawk their wares. Not at all. No one believes in the merits of a home freezer more than I do, but it is up to each of us to decide the way in which our particular freezer can serve us best —when to forget the freezer and take advantage of the best eating in fresh vegetables, what proportion of our vegetable needs to buy from the commercially frozen wares available, and what quantity we choose to freeze at home, from our own garden.

SIX BASIC RULES FOR FREEZING VEGETABLES

1. *Harvesting and selecting.* Choose only well-ripened, tender, choice vegetables in quantities that you can handle with ease. Don't overestimate your energy or time.

2. *Preparing.* Prepare vegetables as you would for the table, but sort them according to size.

3. *Scalding or blanching.* Scald only 1 pound of vegetables at a time in 1 gallon of actively boiling water. Watch scalding time carefully.

4. *Cooling.* Cool immediately in ice water.

5. *Packaging.* Package in moisture-vaporproof materials only.

6. *Freezing.* Freeze immediately, and not too many packages within a 24-hour period.

HARVESTING AND SELECTING

Not all varieties of vegetables are suitable for freezing and the suitable varieties cannot always be adapted to the climatic and soil conditions of your locality. And all vegetables, irrespective of their variety, respond differently to the elements. Some vegetables demand cool, rainy weather if they are going to mature ideally. Others grow to ripe perfection when the weather is warm and balmy. I am listing suitable varieties under the specific directions given for each vegetable. The growing conditions we must leave to nature, but it is a good idea to get the latest variety information from your State agricultural experiment station.

Choose the vegetables for your freezer with utmost care. They are never as perfect as when they are harvested from the garden early in the day. They are at their freshest when the dew is still on the vines and the hot sun has not had the chance to wither or wilt them.

If you don't have your own garden, make overtures to your local farmer or roadside stand owner and get him to harvest the best just for you, at a time when you can pick them up and deal with them the moment you get them into your kitchen. Gather or buy only the quantity that you can prepare and freeze comfortably within 2 hours from the time the vegetables were picked. Never forget that vegetables lose flavor and succulence every minute that they are out of the ground or off the vine.

PREPARING

Speed is essential. Don't waste a moment. Prepare vegetables as carefully as you would for the table. Wash them thoroughly in several changes of cold running water. Discard the overmature or imperfect ones. Sort them according to size so that the scalding will be exact and the packages will be uniform.

Scalding or blanching

If vegetables are not carefully and exactly scalded or blanched, they lose color and develop an off flavor in several weeks.

Scalding retards the action of enzymes, those chemical agents that are present in all living material. Enzymes are essential to the growth and ripening of vegetables, but once maturity is reached and

If vegetables are not carefully and exactly blanched, or scalded, they lose color and develop an off flavor in several weeks. Scalding retards the action of enzymes, those chemical agents that are present in all living material. Vegetables may be scalded in either boiling water or steam.

Westinghouse

STEAM SCALDING. Above: Use a large utensil with a tight-fitting cover. Place a rack in the kettle and add enough water to reach the rack. **Left:** Place 1 pound of prepared vegetables in a fine-mesh wire basket. Place the basket in the kettle, cover tightly, and start counting the scalding time immediately.

COOLING. Vegetables should be cooled immediately after they are scalded to stop further cooking, which might make them mushy. Quick, effective cooling in ice water to 60° F. or lower results in better frozen products.

Westinghouse

DRAIN VEGETABLES THOROUGHLY TO REMOVE EXCESS WATER. Then package them in moisture-vaporproof cartons or bags in the size best suited to your family needs, but be careful not to bruise them. A pint container will yield 3 large or 4 small servings of most vegetables.

the vegetable is harvested, the enzymes speed up the oxidation of the vegetable cells, causing an astoundingly rapid loss of vitamins, color, and flavor.

It is important to understand that scalding does not destroy enzymatic action. It simply retards the work of the organisms that cause spoilage. Storing at zero temperature further discourages the enzymes, yet slowly and inevitably their insidious job of destruction continues. As each month goes by, frozen vegetables will lessen in flavor. Imperceptibly if they are prepared and scalded with care, but no frozen vegetable should be stored longer than from one growing season to another. The sooner they are eaten after freezing, the better they will be.

There are two methods of scalding, one in boiling water, the other in steam:

SCALDING IN BOILING WATER in the home kitchen is generally preferable to steam scalding. Leafy vegetables *must* be scalded in boiling water for uniform results. The flavor of broccoli, on the other hand, is slightly better if the broccoli is steam-scalded.

Some authorities prefer steam scalding. The premise upon which they base their reasoning is that boiling water dissipates vitamins and minerals to a greater extent than steam.

This is not entirely true. We know that heat of any kind is harmful to vitamins, whether it be steam or boiling water. Water of course leaches out the water-soluble vitamins, such as C, and water-soluble minerals. But since all scalded vegetables must be quickly chilled in ice water, this step of the preparation is bound to leach out the small amount of vitamin C and minerals that are preserved in the steam scalding. And since certainly more uniform results are obtained by vegetables being bathed on all sides and agitated in boiling water, scalding in boiling water is the method I prefer. Both are given, and let yours be the preference from your own experience.

WATER SCALDING

Scald only 1 pound of any vegetable at a time in 1 gallon of rapidly boiling water. Larger quantities of vegetables in this amount of water would reduce the temperature of the water so drastically that the exact scalding time listed for each vegetable would be affected and inferior products might result.

Use a large kettle with a tight-fitting cover. Bring 1 gallon of water to a rapid boil, so that when 1 pound of vegetables is added the temperature of the water will not drop more than 10 degrees.

Place 1 pound of vegetables in a fine-mesh wire basket with a lid, or tie them loosely in cheesecloth. Immerse the vegetables in the boiling water, cover tightly, and start counting the scalding time immediately.

Be sure to bring the water back to a vigorous boil each time before adding another pound batch and renew the water with boiling water from a tea kettle as it boils away.

STEAM SCALDING

Use a large utensil with a tight-fitting cover, preferably a pressure cooker with the petcock open. Place a rack in the kettle and add enough water to reach the rack (about 2 or 3 inches) but not touch the vegetables. Keep the water boiling vigorously during the steaming period.

Place 1 pound of prepared vegetables in a fine-mesh wire basket. Place the basket in the kettle, cover tightly, and start counting scalding time as given for individual vegetables. In general, steam scalding time increases water scalding time by one half. A collander with small perforations may be used, or the vegetables can be tied loosely in cheesecloth.

All blanching times are for 1 pound of vegetables. At 5000 feet or more above sea level, scald all vegetables 1 minute longer.

Cooling

Vegetables should be cooled immediately after scalding to stop further cooking, which might make them mushy. Quick, effective cooling to 60° F. or lower results in better frozen products.

Fill the sink, or a large pan, with ice water. Leave the vegetables in the basket or cheesecloth in which they were blanched, lower the basket or cheesecloth in the ice water, and move them back and forth for several minutes, or until thoroughly cool. A good rule is to cool the vegetables for the same length of time as they were blanched. Renew the supply of ice as it melts. Drain thoroughly to remove excess water.

PACKAGING

Package vegetables in moisture-vaporproof cartons or bags in the size that is best suited to your family needs, but be careful not to bruise them. A pint carton will yield 3 large or 4 small servings of most vegetables. A quart container will yield 6 generous or 8 small servings. Containers larger than quarts are not recommended. For a family of two, package vegetables in small bags containing just enough for two servings and enclose several of the small bags in a larger one.

Vegetables expand a little when freezing, but do not require as much headspace as fruits or purées. Leave ½ inch headspace in pint cartons and ¾ inch in quart cartons for tightly packed vegetables. Loosely packed foods such as broccoli or cauliflower need no headspace.

Press out as much of the air as possible from the containers and seal tightly. Wipe the edges of the bag with a dry cloth to remove any moisture that would prevent a complete seal and seal with a warm iron.

Label packaged vegetables clearly with the kind of vegetable, the variety, the date packed, and any special information.

FREEZING

Freeze packaged vegetables as soon as possible. Put them one by one in the refrigerator until all the packages are ready. Then transfer them to the freezing compartment of your freezer. Spread the packages evenly against the freezer plates or coils, but keep them far enough apart from one another so that the air can move between them. After 24 hours, the frozen vegetables may be put in the storage compartments.

COOKING FROZEN VEGETABLES

Whether fresh or frozen, vegetables are best when they are cooked quickly in a tightly covered container, with a small amount of water, until just barely tender. Since frozen vegetables have already been partially cooked, they need only about half the cooking time required for the fresh product. Care should be taken not to overcook them.

With the exception of corn-on-the-cob and spinach and other similar greens, frozen vegetables do not need to be thawed before they are cooked. Simply break the frozen vegetables into several chunks and put the chunks in a saucepan with from ¼ to ½ cup boiling water and a little salt. Cook over a brisk fire until the chunks can be separated with a fork to allow the water and steam to circulate, reduce the heat, and simmer until tender.

If you cook more than one package of a frozen vegetable at a time, use a wide pan so that one package need not be placed upon another. A large skillet with a tight-fitting lid is a perfect cooking kettle and is superior to a deeper saucepan smaller in diameter.

Cook only the amount of vegetables to be eaten at one meal. Large packages may be cut in half with a sharp knife while still frozen and the unused portion wrapped and returned to the freezer.

Beets, squash, pumpkin, sweet potato, and vegetable purées that have been completely cooked before freezing should be heated to serving temperature in a saucepan placed over boiling water.

Partially thaw spinach and other greens. The water that clings to the leaves forms a solid block when frozen. The block should be thawed until it can be broken into chunks, otherwise the outer leaves will be cooked to a mush before the center is thawed.

Corn-on-the-cob must be completely thawed before it is cooked. If frozen ears were dropped into boiling water, the kernels would be cooked before the cobs defrosted. Thaw the ears at room temperature in their wrappings.

Oven-cooked vegetables take longer, but this method is excellent if an oven meal is being prepared.

Break the frozen vegetables into chunks and place the chunks in a buttered casserole. Sprinkle with salt and pepper and dot with bits of butter. Cover the casserole tightly and cook in a moderate oven (350° F.) for 30 minutes. The vegetables are butter-steamed in their own juice.

There are many new and exciting ways to serve vegetables. I wish I could give you most of them, but that is impossible. This is not a book on vegetable cookery; it is a book on freezing and the best I can do, with space limitations, is to suggest a few new ideas. I hope you like them.

Cooking time for vegetables

It is almost impossible to give the exact cooking time for frozen vegetables, as it will vary with the variety and the maturity of the vegetable and the size of the pieces. The amount of water will also vary with the cooking time.

The following is approximate.

2 CUPS OR 1 POUND	AMOUNT OF WATER IN CUPS	TIME OF COOKING AFTER WATER RETURNS TO BOIL IN MINUTES
Asparagus, spears	½ to 1	5 to 8
Asparagus, cut	¼ to ½	3 to 4
Beans, Lima	½ to 1	7 to 15
Beans, green	¼ to 1	10 to 15
Broccoli	¼ to ½	6 to 8
Cauliflower	½	4 to 6
Corn, cut	¼ to ½	5 to 6
Corn-on-the-cob	to cover	4 to 5
Peas	¼ to ½	5 to 7
Soybeans	½ to 1	10 to 15
Spinach	¼ to ½	4 to 6

Details of home-freezing vegetables

ASPARAGUS

Suggested varieties: Mary Washington
Martha Washington
Most garden varieties

1 crate (24 pounds) yields 20 pints
1 to 1¼ pounds yield 1 pint

Harvest, prepare, and freeze within 2 hours.
Avoid using iron utensils, as they discolor asparagus.

Select young, tender asparagus with thick, compact tips.

Wash thoroughly, discard the woody portion of the stalks, and sort into 3 groups according to the thickness of the stalks. The flavor of frozen asparagus is improved if the scales on the stalks are nipped off with a sharp knife, and any sand which lurks under these scales is also eliminated. Leave the stalks in lengths to fit the package, or cut it into 2-inch pieces.

Scald in boiling water or steam with the tips up:

	BOILING WATER	STEAM
Small stalks	2 minutes	4 minutes
Medium stalks	3 minutes	5 minutes
Large stalks	4 minutes	6 minutes

Cool in ice water and drain.
Pack into containers, alternating tip and stem ends.
Seal and freeze.

WAYS TO SERVE:

Serve cooked asparagus with melted butter or hollandaise sauce. Leftover cooked asparagus makes a delicious salad if marinated in the refrigerator for a few hours in French dressing with a sprinkling of finely chopped onion and parsley.

Asparagus au gratin

Arrange stalks of cooked asparagus on thin slices of freshly made toast. Pour over the asparagus a few tablespoons of cream sauce and sprinkle with fine dry bread crumbs mixed with an equal amount of grated cheese. Dot generously with butter and bake in a hot oven (450° F.) until the sauce is bubbling and delicate brown. This makes a delicious luncheon dish.

Asparagus polonaise

Cook 1 pound frozen asparagus according to standard instructions. Sauté ½ cup soft fine bread crumbs in ½ cup hot sweet butter, stirring constantly, until the crumbs are golden brown. Stir in 1 hard-cooked egg, finely chopped, 2 tablespoons finely chopped parsley, and salt and pepper to taste. Arrange the asparagus on a hot serving platter and pour the sauce over it.

BEANS, GREEN OR WAX

Suggested varieties: GREEN: Giant Stringless
Kentucky Wonder
Blue Lake
Tendergreen
WAX: Round Pod Kidney

1 bushel (30 pounds) yields 30 to 40 pints
⅔ to 1 pound yield 1 pint

Avoid using iron utensils, as they discolor beans.

Select only tender, crisp, stringless beans of bright color.

Wash thoroughly; discard immature, bruised, or discolored beans, and sort for size. Cut off stem ends and tips. Leave whole, or cut into 1-inch pieces, or slice lengthwise into thin strips for Frenched beans.

Scald in boiling water or steam:

	BOILING WATER	STEAM
Whole beans	3 minutes	4 minutes
Cut beans	2 minutes	3 minutes
Frenched beans	1 minute	2 minutes

Cool promptly in ice water and drain.
Pack into cartons or bags, leaving ½ inch headspace.
Seal and freeze.

Green beans niçoise

2 onions, thinly sliced
½ green pepper, finely diced
1 cup stewed tomatoes
A bouquet garni of 4 sprigs parsley, 1 stalk celery with the leaves, and 1 bay leaf, all tied together
1 pound French-cut frozen string beans, cooked until barely tender in a small amount of water
3 tablespoons butter
Salt and pepper
1 tablespoon finely chopped parsley

Simmer the onions and green pepper in the tomatoes with the bouquet garni for about 20 minutes, or until the vegetables are tender. Discard the bouquet garni. Toss the string beans with the butter and salt and pepper, pour the tomato sauce over them, and sprinkle with the chopped parsley.

BEANS, LIMA

Suggested varieties: Fordhook Bush
King of the Garden
Baby Fordhook
Burpee Improved
Henderson Bush

1 bushel in the pods (32 pounds) yields 12 to 16 pints
2 to 2½ pounds yield 1 pint

Select young Lima beans with plump pods.
Shell the beans and sort them according to 3 sizes.
Scald in boiling water or steam:

	BOILING WATER	STEAM
Baby beans	1 minute	2 minutes
Medium beans	1½ minutes	2½ minutes
Large beans	2 minutes	3 minutes

Discard any beans that turn white during the scalding, for this means that they are overmature and contain too much starch for a good frozen product.

Cool in ice water and drain.
Pack into pint cartons or bags, leaving ½ inch headspace.
Seal and freeze.

Lima beans in cream

Cook 1 pound frozen Lima beans according to standard instructions. Drain and sprinkle with salt and pepper. Add 2 tablespoons finely chopped parsley and ½ cup heavy cream, cover, and keep the beans hot until ready to serve.

Lima beans and mushrooms

Cook 1 pound frozen Lima beans according to standard instructions. Drain, sprinkle with salt and pepper and combine with 1 cup sliced mushrooms sautéed until tender in butter.

BEET GREENS. See **GREENS**

BEETS

> *Suggested varieties:*   Dark Red
>   Crosby
> · 1 bushel without the tops (52 pounds) yields 35 to 40 pints
> 1¼ to 1½ pounds yield 1 pint

Select deep red, young beets not larger than 3 inches in diameter.
Wash the beets and sort them according to size. Trim the tops,
leaving ½ inch of the stems.
Cook in boiling water until tender:

Small beets	25 to 30 minutes
Medium beets	45 to 50 minutes

Cool in ice water and slip off the skins.
Small beets not over 1½ inches in diameter may be frozen whole.
Larger beets should be sliced or diced or quartered.
Pack in cartons or bags, leaving ½ inch headspace for cut beets.
Whole beets need no headspace.

Glazed beets

Defrost 2 cups precooked, frozen tiny beets over boiling water.
Heat 3 tablespoons butter in a saucepan, add the beets, and shake
them over a moderate flame for about 3 minutes until they are
coated with butter. Sprinkle the beets with 1 tablespoon sugar and
continue to shake the pan for another minute or so, until the beets
are glazed.

Beets with sour cream

Cook 1 pound frozen beets according to standard instructions.
Drain and press them through a fine sieve.

In a saucepan placed over boiling water whisk 1 cup heavy sour cream with 2 tablespoons butter until the mixture is hot and creamy. Add the beet purée, salt, pepper, and a dash of cayenne, and mix thoroughly.

BROCCOLI

Suggested varieties: Italian Green Sprouting
Calabrese
De Cicco

1 crate (25 pounds) yields 24 pints
1 pound yields 1 pint

Select compact, dark green heads with tender stalks.

Soak broccoli for ½ hour in a solution of 4 teaspoons salt dissolved in 1 gallon of cold water to remove any insects. Wash in clear, cold water, discard the large leaves and any tough portion of the stalks, and split the stalks lengthwise, so that the heads are not more than 1½ inches wide.

Scald in boiling water or steam:

BOILING WATER	STEAM
4 minutes	5 minutes

Cool in ice water and drain.

Pack in cartons or bags, arranging the heads in opposite directions. No headspace is necessary. Or wrap in moisture-vaporproof paper and protect the package with an outer wrap of locker tape. Seal and freeze.

WAYS TO SERVE

Serve broccoli hot with *sauce hollandaise* or *mousseline.* Serve it cold with French dressing or *sauce vinaigrette.*

Broccoli amandine

Cook 1 pound frozen broccoli according to standard instructions. Drain the broccoli and arrange it on a warm serving platter. Pour over it ¼ cup butter mixed with 2 tablespoons lemon juice and sprinkle with ½ cup finely shredded toasted almonds.

BRUSSELS SPROUTS

Suggested varieties: Hall Dwarf Improved
                          Long Island Improved
                          Most garden varieties

1 bushel (32 pounds) yields 16 pints
2 pounds yield 1 pint

Select firm, compact, bright green sprouts.

Soak the sprouts for ½ hour in a solution of 4 teaspoons salt dissolved in 1 gallon of cold water to remove any insects. Remove the coarse outer leaves and discard any wilted or discolored sprouts. Wash the sprouts in clear, cold water and sort them into 3 sizes.

Scald in boiling water:

Small heads	3 minutes
Medium heads	4 minutes
Large heads	5 minutes

Cool quickly in cold water and drain.

Pack Brussels sprouts in cartons or bags, allowing 5 to 6 heads per serving, depending on their size. No headspace is necessary.

Seal and freeze.

Brussels sprouts sautéed with grated onion

Cook 1 quart frozen Brussels sprouts according to standard instructions and drain. Melt 4 tablespoons butter in a skillet. Add the Brussels sprouts and 1 tablespoon grated onion and shake the skillet over a moderate flame for 3 minutes. Sprinkle with 2 tablespoons finely chopped parsley and serve.

Brussels sprouts with crisp bacon

Sauté 6 slices of bacon, diced, until crisp and drain on absorbent paper. Pour off all but 2 tablespoons of the fat in the skillet and in the remaining fat sauté 1 small onion, finely chopped, until it is tender. Add 1 quart frozen Brussels sprouts, cooked according to standard instructions and drained, and shake the skillet over the flame for 1 minute. Turn into a serving dish and garnish with the crisp bacon.

CABBAGE

Frozen cabbage is not suitable for use in coleslaw or salads.

Select solid, green heads with crisp leaves.
Discard the coarse outer leaves and cut the head into wedges, or shred rather coarsely.
Scald in boiling water:

Wedges	3 minutes
Shredded cabbage	1½ minutes

Cool in ice water and drain.
Pack cabbage into cartons, leaving ½ inch headspace.
Seal and freeze.

WAYS TO SERVE:
Serve frozen cabbage cooked with caraway seeds and tossed in butter, or . . .

Cabbage sweet and sour

Stew 1 tablespoon finely chopped onion in 2 tablespoons butter and ¼ cup water for 3 minutes. Add 2 cups frozen, shredded cabbage, cover, and cook for 10 minutes. Add 1 sour apple, thinly sliced, ½ teaspoon salt, a little more water if necessary, and simmer for about 10 minutes, or until the cabbage is barely tender. Add 2

tablespoons each red wine and brown sugar and simmer for 5
minutes longer.

CARROTS

> *Suggested varieties:*   Nantes Coreless
>   Red-cored Chantenay
>   Amsterdam Coreless
>   Imperator

> 1 bushel without the tops (50 pounds) yields 40 to 50 pints
> 1 to 1¼ pounds yield 1 pint

Select young, small or medium, bright orange carrots.

Wash the carrots, scrape, and sort for size. Leave the small
carrots whole. Cut the others into ¼-inch cubes, thin slices, or
lengthwise strips.

Scald in boiling water or steam:

	BOILING WATER	STEAM
Whole, small carrots	5 minutes	6 minutes
Lengthwise strips	3 minutes	4 minutes
Diced or sliced carrots	2 minutes	3 minutes

Cool in ice water and drain.

Pack carrots into cartons or bags, leaving ½ inch headspace for
cut carrots. Alternate large and small ends of whole carrots compactly; for these no headspace is necessary.

WAYS TO SERVE:

Serve carrots hot, tossed with butter and plenty of finely chopped
parsley, or cold, marinated in *sauce vinaigrette*.

Glazed whole carrots

Cook 1 pound small whole frozen carrots until barely tender
according to standard instructions. Drain and add ¼ cup butter,
¼ cup brown sugar, and a dash of salt and continue to cook, stirring frequently, until the carrots are glazed and golden.

Carrots and peas

Prepare carrots and peas separately.
Cool and mix them in any desired proportions.
Package and freeze.

CAULIFLOWER

Suggested varieties: Forbes
White Mountain
Perfection
Snowball

12 medium-sized heads (24 pounds) yield 24 pints
1 pound yields 1 pint

Select compact, snow-white heads.

Cut the heads of cauliflower from their thick bases and surrounding leaves and break or cut them into flowerets about 1 inch across.

Soak the pieces for ½ hour in a solution of 4 teaspoons salt dissolved in 1 gallon of cold water; wash in clear, cold water, and drain.

Scald in boiling water or steam:

Boiling water	3 minutes
Steam	5 minutes

Pack compactly into cartons or bags, leaving no headspace.
Seal and freeze.

Cauliflower fritters

Thaw frozen cauliflower and sprinkle the flowerets with salt, pepper, and lemon juice. Dip the flowerets into fritter batter and fry them a few at a time in hot, deep fat until golden. Drain on absorbent paper and serve hot.

Cauliflower polonaise

Cook 1 pound frozen cauliflower according to standard instructions with 1 tablespoon lemon juice and a generous dash of nutmeg. Drain, turn into a serving dish, and pour over it ½ cup fine dry bread crumbs, sautéed in butter until golden. Sprinkle with finely chopped parsley.

CELERY

Select crisp, tender stalks.
Wash celery thoroughly, trim, and cut the stalks into 1-inch lengths.
Scald in boiling water for 3 minutes.
Cool in ice water and drain.
Pack into cartons or bags, leaving ½ inch headspace.
Seal and freeze.

Celery casserole

Cook 1 pound frozen celery according to standard instructions and drain. Stir in 1 cup mornay sauce and turn the celery into a buttered casserole. Sprinkle the celery with fine, dry bread crumbs mixed with 1 tablespoon grated cheese and brown in a hot oven, or under the broiler flame.

Celery parmigiana

Cook 1 pound frozen celery according to standard instructions with 1 small onion, chopped, 1 clove, and 2 slices of bacon, diced, and drain. Put a layer of celery in a buttered shallow casserole, cover it with tomato sauce, and sprinkle with grated Parmesan cheese. Repeat the layers until the celery is used, ending with sauce and cheese. Bake the celery in a hot oven (400° F.) for 10 minutes.

COLLARDS. See GREENS

CORN, WHOLE KERNEL AND CREAM-STYLE

Suggested varieties: Golden Cross
8-Row Golden Bantam
Golden Bantam Hybrids
Golden Bantam
Iona
Seneca Chief
Country Gentleman

1 bushel in the husks (35 pounds) yields 20 to 24 pints

Select freshly picked sweet corn with full, regular kernels. The kernels should be golden and shiny and when one is ruptured with the thumb nail, the milk should spurt out.

Husk the ears, remove the silk, and wash the corn.

Scald the corn-on-the-cob in boiling water for 4 to 5 minutes.

Cool the corn in ice water and drain.

For WHOLE KERNEL CORN, cut the kernels from the cob close to the cob. For CREAM-STYLE CORN, cut the corn from the cobs at about the center of the kernels. Scrape the cob with the back of the knife to remove the heart of the kernel and the corn juice.

Package in cartons or bags, leaving ½ inch headspace.

Seal and freeze.

WAYS TO SERVE:

In a saucepan, combine 2 cups frozen whole kernel corn, ¾ cup heavy cream, 1 tablespoon paprika, salt, and a pinch of cayenne. Cover the saucepan and cook the corn over boiling water for about 20 minutes, or until the corn is thawed and the mixture is steaming hot. Stir in 2 tablespoons sweet butter and serve.

Corn pudding

Thaw 2 cups cream-style frozen corn and mix it with 1 cup cream, salt, pepper, and 2 tablespoons melted butter. Stir in 3 lightly beaten egg yolks and fold in 3 egg whites, stiffly beaten. Turn the pudding into a buttered baking dish and bake in a moderate oven (350° F.) for 40 minutes.

CORN-ON-THE-COB

Suggested varieties: Golden Cross Bantam
8-Row Golden Bantam
Golden Midget

Don't expect frozen corn-on-the-cob to taste like the garden-fresh vegetable. It doesn't.

Select only the most tender, succulent ears.
Husk the ears and remove the silk, wash the corn, and sort it according to sizes.
Scald in boiling water:

Small ears 1¼ inches or less in diameter	6 minutes
Medium ears 1¼ to 1½ inches in diameter	8 minutes
Large ears over 1½ inches in diameter	10 minutes

Cool immediately and thoroughly in ice water and drain.
Wrap each ear in moisture-vaporproof paper, seal, and freeze.
When frozen, several ears may be tidily packed in a bag, a carton, or stockinette.

WAYS TO SERVE:
Thaw corn-on-the-cob for 2 hours at room temperature in the unopened wrappings. Drop into boiling water, cover, and simmer for 10 minutes.

EGGPLANT

Suggested varieties: Black Beauty
New York Purple
Any good garden variety

1 bushel (33 pounds) yields 33 pints
1 pound yields 1 pint

Select firm, ripe eggplant about 6 inches in diameter.
Overmature eggplant is not good for freezing.

Peel one eggplant at a time, cut it into slices ½ inch thick, and drop the slices into a solution of 3 teaspoons lemon juice and 1 quart water. Work quickly to prevent discoloration.

Blanch the slices in boiling water or steam:

Boiling water	4 minutes
Steam	5 minutes

Cool in 1 gallon of ice water to which is added the juice of 1 lemon. Rinse in ice water and drain.

Reshape the eggplant, putting two pieces of freezer paper between the slices. Wrap the reshaped eggplant in moisture-vapor-proof paper.

Seal and freeze.

Eggplant parmigiana

1 large eggplant, thawed in its wrappings
1 cup olive oil
1½ cups tomato sauce
4 tablespoons grated Parmesan cheese
½ pound Mozzarella cheese, thinly sliced

Drain the eggplant slices on absorbent paper and sauté them in the hot olive oil until they are brown on both sides. Drain them again on absorbent paper.

Place a layer of the eggplant in a casserole and cover it with some of the tomato sauce. Sprinkle the sauce with some of the Parmesan and cover with a layer of the Mozzarella. Repeat the layers until all the eggplant is used, ending with Mozzarella. Bake in a hot oven (400° F.) for 15 minutes.

Deep-fried eggplant

Thaw the eggplant in its wrapping. Dip the slices in fritter batter and fry as you would the fresh vegetable.

GREENS
(beet greens, collards, kale, mustard greens, spinach, Swiss chard, turnip greens)

Suggested varieties:

> BEET GREENS AND COLLARDS: Any good garden varieties
> KALE: Dwarf Green Curled
> MUSTARD GREENS: Florida Broadleaf, Southern Giant, Mammoth
> SPINACH: King of Denmark, Nobel, Longstanding Bloomsdale, Bloomsdale Savoy
> SWISS CHARD: Fordhook, Lucullus

1 bushel (12 pounds) of collards, mustard greens, Swiss chard, or turnip greens yields 12 to 14 pints
1 bushel (15 pounds) of beet greens yields 15 pints
1 bushel (18 pounds) of kale or spinach yields 18 to 20 pints

Select young, tender greens.

Discard the bruised and imperfect leaves and cut off the tough stems before washing. Wash the greens thoroughly in several changes of cold water to remove all the sand.

Scald only ½ pound at a time in 1 gallon boiling water. Twirl the container several times during the scalding to separate the leaves.

Beet greens, kale, mustard greens, turnip greens, Swiss chard, spinach	2 minutes
Collards	3 minutes

Cool immediately in ice water and drain.

Pack greens into cartons or bags, leaving ½ inch headspace. Do not press greens compactly into containers.

Seal and freeze.

WAYS TO SERVE:

Beet greens, mustard greens, collards, and Swiss chard are best cooked according to standard instructions, drained, and tossed with salt, pepper, and butter. Kale is delicious tossed with diced bacon, sautéed until crisp. Add 1 small onion, finely chopped, to the water in which the frozen kale is cooked. Spinach is excellent cooked and served as a spinach *soufflé,* or cooked in the following ways . . .

Spinach Parmesan

Cook 1 pound of frozen spinach according to standard instructions and drain. Add ¼ cup butter, salt and pepper to taste, a pinch of nutmeg, and 3 tablespoons grated Parmesan cheese and mix well.

Spinach purée

Cook 1 pound of frozen spinach according to standard instructions and drain. Rub the spinach through a fine sieve and mix the purée with 1 cup rich cream sauce. Season the mixture with salt, pepper, and nutmeg and keep hot over boiling water until serving time.

KALE. See GREENS

KOHLRABI

> *Suggested varieties:* Early White Vienna
> Any good garden variety

Select young, mild-flavored, small to medium-sized kohlrabi.
Discard the tops and roots of kohlrabi. Wash and peel.
The small roots may be left whole, or all may be cut into ½-inch cubes.
Scald in boiling water or steam:

	BOILING WATER	STEAM
Whole kohlrabi	3 minutes	5 minutes
Cubes	2 minutes	3 minutes

Cool in ice water and drain.
Pack whole kohlrabi into cartons or bags, or wrap in moisture-vaporproof paper. Pack cubes into cartons or bags, leaving ½ inch headspace.
Seal and freeze.

WAYS TO SERVE:
Serve kohlrabi hot, mixed with cream sauce, or cold, marinated in French dressing or *sauce vinaigrette*.

MUSHROOMS

> 10 pounds yield 20 pints

Select fresh, white, cultivated mushrooms.
Wash the mushrooms briefly. If they are white they will need little washing. Wiping with a damp cloth is sufficient. Discard the

tough portion of the stems. Sort according to size. Leave whole the small button mushrooms not larger than 1 inch across. Slice the rest.

Sauté ½ pound mushrooms at a time in 4 tablespoons hot butter for 4 to 5 minutes, or until almost cooked. Turn them into a flat dish and cool them over cracked ice.

Or soak the mushrooms for 5 minutes in a solution of 1 tablespoon lemon juice and 6 cups cold water.

Steam:

Whole mushrooms not larger than 1 inch across	5 minutes
Tiny buttons, or quartered mushrooms	3 minutes
Sliced mushrooms	4 minutes

Cool promptly in ice water and drain.

Pack in cartons or bags, leaving ½ inch headspace in the packages containing the sliced mushrooms.

Seal and freeze.

Mushrooms in cream

1 scallion, chopped
1 small onion, chopped
2 tablespoons butter
2 tablespoons olive oil
1 pound frozen, sliced mushrooms
Salt and pepper
½ cup heavy cream

Sauté the scallion and onion in the oil and butter until the onion is golden in color. Add the mushrooms, sprinkle with salt and pepper, cover, and cook over a low flame for 15 minutes. Add the cream and continue to cook for 3 minutes longer, stirring constantly.

MUSTARD GREENS. See GREENS

OKRA

Suggested varieties: Clemson Spineless
White Lightning
Dwarf Green

Select tender, young, green pods.

Wash thoroughly, rinse, and sort for size. Cut off the stems without cutting into the seed cells, as this would let the juices leak out during the scalding.

Scald in boiling water:

Small pods	3 minutes
Large pods	4 minutes

Cool in ice water and drain.

Leave whole or sliced crosswise.

Pack compactly in cartons or bags, alternating top and tip ends, leaving ½ inch headspace.

Seal and freeze.

WAYS TO SERVE:

Cook frozen okra and serve it with lemon and butter or creamed. It may be sautéed or French fried, or combined with onion, corn, and tomatoes in a stew.

Okra au gratin

1 pound frozen okra
1½ cups cream sauce
¼ cup bread crumbs
1½ tablespoons butter
¼ cup grated Parmesan cheese

Cook the okra according to standard directions, drain, and turn it into a buttered baking dish. Pour the cream sauce over the okra, sprinkle with bread crumbs, dot with butter, and sprinkle with the cheese. Bake in a moderate oven (375° F.) for about 20 minutes, or until the sauce is bubbling and the crumbs are brown.

PARSLEY

Not suitable for garnish, as frozen parsley becomes limp when it thaws.

Select fresh, deep green curly or Italian parsley.

Wash and discard the stems.

Package small quantities of the clusters in tiny bags made by heat-sealing freezer paper on three sides. Pack several bags in one carton.

Seal and freeze.

To use: Chop parsley while it is still frozen for use in stews, casseroles, croquettes, sauces, and other cooked dishes.

PARSNIPS

Suggested varieties: Hollow Crown
Marrowfat

1 bushel (50 pounds) yields 40 to 50 pints

Select young, small to medium-sized parsnips with a small center core.

Discard tops, wash, and peel. Cut lengthwise into ¼-inch-thick strips or cut into ½-inch cubes or slices.

Scald in boiling water for 2 minutes.

Cool in ice water and drain.

Pack in cartons or bags, leaving ½ inch headspace.

Seal and freeze.

Parsnip croquettes

Cook 1 pound of frozen parsnips in a small amount of boiling salted water with 1 teaspoon sugar in a tightly covered saucepan until tender but not mushy. Put the parsnips through a ricer and add enough hot cream to make a thick purée. Stir in 2 egg yolks, lightly beaten, and 2 tablespoons melted butter, and correct the seasoning. Spread the mixture on a platter to cool. Form it into small croquettes. Dip the croquettes in flour, then in 1 egg beaten with 1 tablespoon milk and 1 tablespoon olive oil, and then in fine dry bread crumbs.

Fry the croquettes in hot, deep fat or sauté them in butter until golden. Drain on absorbent paper and serve on a hot platter decorated with fried parsley.

PEAS, GREEN

Suggested varieties: Thomas Laxton
Dark Podded Thomas Laxton
Improved Gradus
Little Marvel
Alderman

1 bushel in the pods (30 pounds) yields 12 to 15 pints
2 to 2½ pounds yield 1 pint

Harvest early in the morning and freeze within 1 hour from the vine.

Select young, bright green, plump pods with sweet, tender peas.

Shell the peas, discarding any overmature, immature, or wrinkled peas.

Scald in boiling water or steam:

Boiling water	1½ minutes
Steam	2 minutes

Cool promptly in ice water and drain.
Package in cartons or bags, leaving ½ inch headspace.
Seal and freeze.

WAYS TO SERVE:

Peas are at their best when they are cooked in a small amount of salted water and tossed with butter and parsley and, if you like, a little heavy cream. They may be combined with mushrooms or tiny whole cooked onions and cream sauce, or served sprinkled with finely chopped fresh mint.

Peas French style

1 pound frozen peas
8 tender lettuce leaves, shredded
10 small white onions
1 teaspoon sugar
¼ cup water
Salt and pepper
Butter

In a saucepan or baking dish put the peas, lettuce leaves, onions, sugar, and water. Cover the dish tightly and cook the peas gently for about 15 minutes, or until tender. Season with salt and pepper, add a good lump of butter, and serve hot.

PEPPERS, SWEET

Suggested varieties: California Wonder
Windsor
Oakview Wonder

1 bushel (25 pounds) yields 20 quarts (21 pounds)
3 peppers (⅔ pound) yield 1 pint

Select firm, crisp, brightly colored peppers with glossy skin and thick walls, uniformly deep green.

Wash peppers thoroughly, cut out stems, and remove the seeds.

Leave whole or cut into ½-inch strips or rings, or halve, or slice or dice according to use.

Scald peppers in boiling water or steam:

	BOILING WATER	STEAM
Whole or halves	3 minutes	4 minutes
Slices or dice	2 minutes	3 minutes

Cool in ice water and drain.

Pack in cartons or bags, leaving ½ inch headspace, or pack small amounts in envelopes made by heat-sealing freezer paper on three sides, then package several envelopes in pint cartons or bags.

Seal and freeze.

Peppers Roman style

Sauté 1 small onion, sliced, in 1 tablespoon of butter and 1 tablespoon olive oil until the onion is golden. Add 3 tomatoes, peeled and chopped, or 1 cup stewed tomatoes and cook for 5 minutes. Add 1 pound frozen, sliced peppers and salt and pepper to taste. Cover the skillet and cook the peppers slowly for 30 minutes, stirring frequently.

PIMIENTOS

Suggested variety: Perfection

Select crisp, thick-walled, deep red pimientos.

Roast the pimientos in a hot oven (400° F.) for 3 to 4 minutes and wash off the charred skins under cold running water.

Follow instructions given for Sweet Peppers.

Pack pimientos into cartons or bags, leaving ½ inch headspace. Seal and freeze.

Thaw pimientos for use in salads and sandwich fillings, or as a garnish.

POTATOES, FRENCH FRIED

Do not store longer than 6 weeks.

Select uniform potatoes.

Peel, wash, and cut them lengthwise into ¼-inch-thick slices. Cut across the slices at ¼-inch intervals to make regular julienne strips. Soak the strips in cold water for 5 minutes, drain, and dry them on a towel. Fry the potato strips in hot deep fat (370° F.) until they are pale gold. Drain on absorbent paper.

Spread the fried potatoes in a flat pan and chill them over cracked ice.

Package compactly in cartons, leaving ½ inch headspace.

Cool and freeze.

WAYS TO SERVE:

Remove the pale gold frozen potatoes from the carton and plunge them into deep hot fat (400° F.) for 2 minutes. Or place them on a cookie sheet and bake them in a hot oven (425° F.) for 15 to 20 minutes, basting them several times with a little melted butter.

POTATOES, SWEET

Suggested varieties: Puerto Rico
Nancy Hall

10 pounds yield 16 pints

Do not store over 3 months.

Bake large sweet potatoes in a moderate oven (350° F.) for 1 to 1½ hours, or until tender.

Cool the potatoes, peel them, and cut into halves or quarters, or slice them ½ inch thick. Dip the slices in lemon juice and roll them in brown sugar.

Pack the potatoes flat, with a double layer of freezer paper between them.

Or mash the potatoes and mix the purée with 2 tablespoons lemon juice or ¼ cup orange juice per pint. Package in moisture-vaporproof containers, leaving 1 inch headspace.

Seal and freeze.

Candied sweet potatoes

Remove potato slices from their container and spread them on a generously buttered shallow pan. Dot each slice with butter, sprinkle with a little salt and pepper, and bake in a moderate oven (350° F.) for about 30 minutes. Or sauté the slices a few at a time in hot butter until they are brown and the sugar is caramelized. Blaze with warm rum or cognac, if desired.

PUMPKIN

Suggested varieties: All deep yellow pie pumpkins
Connecticut Field
Small Sugar

10 pounds yield 12 pints

Select full-colored mature pie pumpkins.

Wash, cut into quarters and discard the seeds and stringy fibers. Place the quarters in a low-sided baking pan containing ½ inch hot water and bake in a moderate oven (350° F.) for about 40 minutes, or until tender. Remove the pulp from the rind and mash or rub it through a sieve or food mill.

Cool the pumpkin purée in a pan placed over cracked ice, stirring occasionally.

Pack into cartons or bags, leaving ½ inch headspace.

Seal and freeze.

Pumpkin pie mix

Pumpkin pie mix may be prepared according to your favorite recipe and frozen within a pie shell, or in a moisture-vaporproof, liquid-tight container. If the latter, save freezer space by leaving out the milk and cream from the recipe. This can be easily added when the mix is thawed.

RUTABAGAS

Suggested varieties: Long Island Improved
American Purple Top

Select young, medium-sized rutabagas.
Cut off the tops, wash, and peel. Cut into ½-inch cubes.
Scald in boiling water for 2 minutes.
Cool in ice water and drain.
Or cook in boiling water until tender. Drain and mash, or rub through a sieve or food mill and cool by stirring the purée in a saucepan over ice water.
Pack in cartons or bags, leaving ½ inch headspace.
Seal and freeze.

WAYS TO SERVE:
Cook cubed rutabagas according to standard instructions and toss with salt, pepper, butter, and parsley. They are also good tossed with diced bacon, sautéed until crisp and golden.
Thaw the rutabaga purée in a saucepan placed over boiling water and whip it until smooth with cream, butter, and salt and pepper to taste. Or combine the rutabaga purée with an equal amount of fluffy mashed potatoes.

SAUERKRAUT

Pack into containers.
Seal and freeze.

SOYBEANS

Suggested varieties: Giant Green
Bansei
Easy Cook
Emperor
Sausei

Select bright green, plump pods.
Wash the pods and drain.
Scald the beans in the pods in boiling water for 5 minutes.
Cool in ice water and squeeze the soybeans out of their pods.
Pack in cartons or bags, leaving ½ inch headspace.
Seal and freeze.

WAYS TO SERVE:
Cook soybeans according to standard instructions and serve them hot, tossed with butter and salt and pepper, or cold, marinated in French dressing.

SPINACH: See GREENS

SQUASH, SUMMER

Suggested varieties: Summer Crookneck
Zucchini
1 bushel (40 pounds) yields 32 to 40 pints
1 to 1¼ pounds yield 1 pint

Select young squash with tender skin and small seeds.
Wash the squash thoroughly and cut them into ½-inch-thick slices or cubes.

Cook 1 pound squash in ½ cup water, without salt or seasonings, in a tightly covered saucepan for 5 minutes, or until tender. There should be little or no water left in the saucepan when the squash is cooked.

Cool by placing the saucepan over cracked ice and stir frequently. The squash may be mashed if desired.

Package in cartons or bags, leaving ½ inch headspace. Seal and freeze.

Or dip sliced squash or zucchini into lemon juice and roll in fine dry bread crumbs. Sauté the slices in hot melted butter until very pale gold and tender. Package the slices in layers in a carton, separating each layer with two layers of freezer paper.

Seal and freeze.

Zucchini sauté

Remove squash slices from the carton and sauté them slowly in hot butter until brown. Sprinkle with salt, pepper, and freshly chopped parsley.

Zucchini casserole

1 pound frozen, sliced zucchini
4 tablespoons butter
1½ cups cream sauce
2 eggs, lightly beaten
2 tablespoons grated Parmesan cheese
Salt and pepper

Sauté the zucchini slices in the butter until they are golden on both sides. Combine the cream sauce, eggs, cheese, and salt and pepper to taste and fold in the zucchini. Turn the mixture into a buttered casserole and bake in a moderate oven (375° F.) for 30 minutes.

SQUASH, WINTER

Suggested varieties: Golden Delicious
Golden Hubbard
Buttercup
Greengold
10 pounds yield 12 pints

Select mature, hard-shelled varieties with firm flesh.

Cut or break the squash into pieces and discard the seeds and stringy fibers. Place the pieces in a shallow-sided baking pan containing ½ inch hot water and bake in a moderate oven (350° F.) for about 40 minutes, or until tender.

Or cook 1 pound squash in ½ cup water in a tightly covered container for 20 minutes, or until tender.

Scrape the pulp from the rind and mash, or rub through a sieve or food mill.

Cool the purée by placing it in a saucepan over cracked ice and stir frequently.

Pack in cartons or bags, leaving ½ inch headspace.

Seal and freeze.

WAYS TO SERVE:

Thaw squash purée in a saucepan placed over boiling water, season with salt and pepper and butter, and serve as a vegetable.

The thawed purée may also be used to good advantage in pies, puddings, and soups.

Hubbard squash purée

Thaw 2 cups squash purée over boiling water and beat into it 2 tablespoons melted butter, 2 teaspoons brown sugar, ¼ teaspoon ground ginger, and salt to taste. Beat in enough hot heavy cream to make a fluffy mixture. Turn into a serving dish and sprinkle with chopped parsley.

SUCCOTASH

Prepare corn and Lima beans separately.
Cool and mix in equal proportions.
Package and freeze.

SWISS CHARD. See GREENS

TOMATO JUICE. See FRUIT JUICES

TURNIPS

Suggested varieties: Purple Top White Globe
Purple Top Strapleaf

Select small or medium-sized firm, tender turnips with a mild flavor.

Remove tops, wash the turnips, peel them, and cut into ½-inch cubes.

Scald in boiling water or steam:

Boiling water	2½ minutes
Steam	3½ minutes

Cool in ice water and drain.
Pack in cartons or bags, leaving ½ inch headspace.
Seal and freeze.

WAYS TO SERVE:

Cook 1 pound frozen turnips according to standard instructions. Drain them well and turn into a skillet containing 3 tablespoons hot butter. Cook the turnips for a few minutes, stirring constantly, then sprinkle them with 1 tablespoon sugar and continue to cook, stirring, until the turnips are nicely glazed.

Or mash cooked turnips and put them in a casserole. Sprinkle generously with grated Parmesan cheese, and brown under the broiler flame.

TURNIP GREENS. See GREENS

VEGETABLE PURÉES

When you are preparing vegetables for freezing you can, if you wish, cook some until tender and purée them for baby food or for cream soups.

Puréed squash, pumpkin, and sweet potato are all excellent for pies. Tomato purée can be used in many ways: in soups, tomato sauces, gravies, and casseroles.

Package purées in quantities to suit your various needs. Baby foods may be frozen in paper cups or ice-cube trays, then wrapped in moisture-waterproof paper, and stored. Small amounts of tomato purée may also be frozen in the same way.

CHAPTER SIX

Fruits, fruit purées, and fruit juices

Of all the foods which freeze well, fruits win the blue ribbon. Freezing, better than any other method of preservation, captures the tree- or vine-ripened fresh flavor of fruits, so essential a part of a healthful diet, and retains their bright color and firm texture. Happily, no other home method of preservation is as easy as freezing fruits.

Whole fruits, fruit juices, and purées are unusually easy to pack for year-round use in desserts and salads and for cold drinks, puddings, ice cream, and ice-cream toppings. And even, if you wish, for jelly- and jam-making *in midwinter,* when there is more time for creative homemaking than during the carefree summer and busy, holiday-packed fall and early winter months.

Fruits need no scalding, but are simply packed in sugar sirup or with dry sugar, or sometimes they require nothing added at all. They may be served while they are still frosty from the freezer.

Fruits are such delightfully superior foods both to eye and palate that it is very hard to restrict oneself to the space limitations of a freezer. If your freezer is a small one, you may wish to store only the fruits that your family are especially fond of. Or you might choose to freeze some of the more exotic fruits that reach our markets at various times of the year, such as persimmons, papaya, or fresh figs, which are not packed by commercial freezing companies, depending upon the reliable frozen food companies to supply your daily needs of orange juice, strawberries, peaches, raspberries, apples, et cetera.

Almost all fruits, including berries and melons, can be successfully frozen, but some freeze better than others. And certain varieties of fruits retain their flavor, color, and texture in freezing better than other varieties. Some of the better known varieties are listed with the detailed instructions for preparing each fruit, but your State agricultural experiment station or your local seed houses can give you information on the fruit varieties grown in your locality that are best suited to home freezing.

SELECTION IS IMPORTANT

Fruits ripened on the bush or tree or vine have more flavor and better color for freezing. Select or pick the fruits that are fully ripe, yet firm. Overripe fruits will freeze to a mush and those that are not ripe enough lack flavor and sweetness. And be sure to taste fruits before you buy them. Blushing peaches and luscious ripe-red berries may look beautiful and yet be watery and tasteless to the bite.

PREPARATION

Fruits and berries lose quality very quickly if they are allowed to stand at room temperature for any length of time. If a delay is unavoidable, store them on trays in the refrigerator until the first free moments. Even then, don't keep the fruits waiting too long for frozen storage.

Work with a small amount of fruit at a time. Clean and sort it carefully and very gently, for all fruits bruise easily. Discard all parts that are blemished, overripe, or green. Wash the fruit carefully in cold running water. It should not be allowed to soak in water, for berries, in particular, will readily exchange valuable and flavorful juice for water. The juices will leach out and water will fill the cells, dissipating the wonderful fruit flavor. Extremely cold water or ice water is best for washing fruit. It helps to prevent "water logging" and keeps the fruit firm. Drain off all the excess water and stem, pit, peel, hull, or slice fruit in exactly the same manner as you would prepare it for the table.

Larger fruits are generally sliced before they are packed. Berries may be left whole, sliced, or crushed. Many fruits can be made into purée or juice.

With only a few exceptions, fruits and berries are packed for freezing either mixed with dry sugar or covered with a sugar syrup. The amount of sugar used depends on the tartness of the fruit, the way you plan to serve it, and personal taste.

Fruits may be packed without sugar or sugar syrup, but usually they are not so satisfactory. For fruits, like vegetables, contain chemical substances called enzymes that continue their work of destruction after the product is harvested. While vegetables are scalded to retard the enzymatic action, fruits are packed with sugar. The sugar performs the same service to fruits as the boiling-water bath does to vegetables—it slows down the action of the enzymes. In addition to this the syrup, whether it is prepared and poured over the fruit or formed by the juice drawn from the fruit combining with the dry sugar, keeps the air away from the fruit and retards oxidation.

Dry pack

The few exceptions to the sugar-pack rule in freezing fruits are: cranberries, boysenberries, gooseberries, loganberries, raspberries, currants, youngberries, and rhubarb. These are fruits that can be washed and prepared without danger of rupturing the skin and that do not darken easily upon exposure to the air. The dry-pack method of packing fruit is usually used for fruits that are to be made into pies, puddings, or preserves.

Wash the fruit carefully and sort it, cutting away any bruises or blemishes and discarding any fruit that is overmature or underripe. Drain the fruit thoroughly between layers of absorbent paper to remove surface moisture and to prevent the fruit from freezing in a solid mass.

Pack the fruit in moisture-vaporproof containers, leaving ½ inch headspace, and seal tightly. Label each package with the name of the fruit, the date of storage, and the way it is to be used, and freeze.

Dry sugar pack

Fruits packed in dry sugar are excellent for making into pies or for other cooking purposes because they are less liquid. And yet this method should not be used for fruits that discolor readily. It is especially suitable for juicy fruits that are sliced or crushed, as the natural fruit juices quickly blend with the sugar to form a protective syrup.

Wash the fruit carefully, sort, and drain it. Prepare the fruit as you would for the table. Work with a small amount of fruit at a time. Spread about 1 quart of fruit in a large, flat pan and sift sugar over it, distributing it as evenly as possible. Four parts of fruit to 1 part of sugar by weight or volume gives adequate protection and is not too sweet for most palates and purposes. The sugar may vary, however, according to the tartness of the fruit. Anywhere from 3 to 5 parts of fruit to 1 part of sugar is the recommended proportion.

Fruit and sugar are best measured by a kitchen scale, but lacking this, the weight must be estimated on the basis that 1 cup tightly packed fruit weighs about as much as 1 cup sugar. For a 4-to-1 pack, then, you should measure 4 cups or 1 quart tightly packed fruit to 1 cup sugar.

Mix the sugar through the fruit gently with a wooden spoon until each piece is coated with sugar.

The sugar may be added to the fruit as the fruit is packed. Fill the package about ¼ full and sprinkle in ¼ of the sugar. Continue to fill the container in this way, shaking the container occasionally to distribute the sugar through the fruit.

Package sugared fruits in liquid-tight, moisture-vaporproof containers, leaving ½ inch headspace. Be certain that the top seal on the bags is complete so there is no danger of the juice leaking out. Label with the name of the fruit, the date of storage, and quantity of sugar added, and the way in which you propose to use it. Freeze and store.

FREEZING STRAWBERRIES.
Work with a small amount of
berries at a time. Clean and sort
them carefully and gently, for
all fruits bruise easily. **Right:**
Wash strawberries in cold running water. They should not be
allowed to soak in the water,
for they will readily exchange
valuable flavorful juice for
water. Extremely cold water
helps to keep the fruit firm.
Below: Drain off all the excess
water and stem the berries.

Westinghouse

International Harvester

Slice the strawberries into a
flat dish and crush them lightly
if desired. Sprinkle them with 1
cup sugar to 4 cups berries, distributing the sugar as evenly as
possible, and toss the berries
with a wooden spoon until they
are thoroughly coated.

Above: Chill oranges or grapefruit in the refrigerator. Peel them, removing all the white skin, and cut the sections free from the membranes. Discard the seeds. Sections may be packaged in combination with other fruits, if desired. **Below:** Cut pineapple into slices ¾ inch thick, remove the outer skin and the eyes from each slice, and cut out the core. Separate the slices with two layers of freezer paper so they may be easily separated while they are still frozen.

Syrup pack

Syrup pack is used for packing fruits that have little juice of their own and is especially valuable for those particular fruits, such as peaches, apricots, plums, and pears, that quickly discolor when the flesh is exposed to the air.

Forty per cent sugar syrup is generally sweet enough for any fruit; however, a higher or lower percentage may be used according to individual taste. A less sweet syrup is better for mild-flavored fruits such as cantaloupe balls or pineapple wedges, because the sugar does not mask the delicate flavor, while a heavier syrup may be preferred for very sour fruits such as sour cherries.

Place the prepared fruit in liquid-tight, moisture-vaporproof containers and cover it with syrup, leaving ¾ inch headspace for expansion during freezing. Each pint of fruit will require about ⅔ cup of syrup.

SUGAR SYRUPS

Add the required amount of sugar to clear, cold water and stir until the sugar is completely dissolved. Keep the syrup in the refrigerator until ready to use, but do not store for longer than 2 days.

PERCENTAGE OF SYRUP	AMOUNT OF SUGAR	AMOUNT OF WATER
20% (very light)	1 cup	4 cups
30% (light)	2 cups	4 cups
40% (medium)	3 cups	4 cups
50% (heavy)	4 cups	4 cups
60% (very heavy)	6 cups	4 cups

Part of the sugar used to make a sugar syrup may be replaced by white corn syrup. As a matter of fact, many fruits are superior in flavor packed in the sugar and corn syrup mixture rather than in all-sugar syrup. Dissolve the sugar in the water, add the corn syrup, and mix well.

HOW TO PREPARE SYRUP
WITH CORN SYRUP AND SUGAR

PERCENTAGE OF SYRUP	AMOUNT OF SUGAR	AMOUNT OF CORN SYRUP	AMOUNT OF WATER
40% (medium)	2 cups	2 cups	5 cups
50% (heavy)	3 cups	2 cups	4 cups

Honey may also be used to replace ¼ of the sugar in the syrup for freezing fruit, but the honey will impart a distinctive flavor to the fruit and should be used only if the family likes honey flavor, as it may mask the flavor of the fruit.

Controlling discoloration

Many of the light-colored tree fruits such as apples, peaches, pears, apricots, and nectarines have a tendency to turn dark when their cut surfaces are exposed to the oxygen in the air during preparation or frozen storage, or, more frequently, when the fruit is thawed. This can be partially prevented by slicing the peeled fruit directly into a container partly filled with syrup. But the most effective way to prevent discoloration is by the use of ascorbic acid.

HOW TO USE ASCORBIC ACID

Ascorbic acid is actually another name for vitamin C, which is one of the major vitamins essential to good health. It not only prevents fruit from oxidizing, but enriches its vitamin C content. Ascorbic acid may be purchased from your drugstore in powdered or crystalline form and is better than tablets, which contain a filler. To use ascorbic acid, simply add it to the syrup just before the syrup is combined with the fruit. Stir only enough to dissolve the powder and stir gently to avoid mixing air into the syrup. Use 1 teaspoon ascorbic acid in 1 quart of prepared syrup.

To use ascorbic acid with dry sugar packs, dissolve ¼ teaspoon ascorbic acid in 2 tablespoons cold water and drip the solution over the fruit before adding the sugar.

HOW TO USE CITRIC ACID OR LEMON JUICE

An alternative method to the ascorbic-acid treatment of fruit is in the use of citric acid or lemon juice, but it is less effective than ascorbic acid and adds tartness to the fruit. Citric acid in powder or crystals is available at your drugstore.

Dissolve 1 teaspoon citric acid in 1 gallon of cold water and immerse the sliced fruit in this solution for 1 minute. Drain the fruit well before packing it, whether with dry sugar or in sugar syrup. Three tablespoons lemon juice may be substituted for the citric acid.

HOW TO USE SODIUM SULPHITE

Of all the fruits that discolor quickly when exposed to the air, apples are probably the worst offenders. The use of sulphur to prevent the rapid browning of the cut surfaces has been known for many years, in the preservation of apples by drying or dehydration. It is used now in freezing apples, and it is unfortunate that the flavor of sulphur can be detected in the thawed product if it is not used discreetly and accurately.

Ask your druggist to give you chemically pure sodium sulphite or sodium bisulphite. Put 1 gallon of cold water in an earthenware, glass, stainless-steel, or enameled container. Add 1½ teaspoons of either sodium sulphite or sodium bisulphite and stir until the chemical is dissolved. Add sliced apples, weigh them down with a plate to keep them submerged in the solution, and let them soak for 5 minutes. Drain immediately. The same solution can be used to treat three or four batches of apples.

Packaging fruit

Heavily waxed tubs with snap-in lids, cartons with Cellophane or plastic liners, or glass jars are all good for packaging fruits. But the containers, no matter what you use, must be not only moisture-vaporproof, to prevent air leakage that would destroy the quality and appearance of the fruit, but liquid-tight, so none of the juice can escape.

Select the size container that is best suited to your needs. A quart-size container will supply fruit for a well-filled 9-inch pie. A quart of strawberries or peaches will make 4 generous individual or 1 large shortcake. If used as an ice-cream or pudding topping, 1 pint of fruit will serve from 4 to 6 people.

Pack the fruit firmly into the container, but don't use enough pressure to crush the fruit that you want to remain whole, and leave ½ inch headspace for dry packs and ¾ inch headspace for syrup packs.

Seal the packages tightly and label each package, with either waterproof ink or a china marking pencil, with the name of the fruit, the date of storage, the quantity of sugar or the percentage of syrup added to the fruit, and the intended use.

FRUIT JUICES

Most fruit juices, including cranberry, cherry, grape, raspberry and strawberry, apple, and citrus and tomato juice, make excellent frozen products and retain their fresh flavor from one season to another. They make refreshing drinks thawed and served cold, or they can be made into fruit sauces, ice creams, and sherbets, or boiled up with sugar and made into clear and sparkling jelly.

Orange and Grapefruit need only be squeezed to extract the juice. The juice is then packed into liquid-tight containers and frozen. Select fully ripe fruit and chill it thoroughly in the refrigerator. Cut the fruit in half, ream out the juice, and strain it through a stainless steel or plastic strainer or cheesecloth. Pour the juice into the containers, leaving 1 inch headspace, and freeze immediately.

Apples as well as citrus fruits need no heat treatment. Extract the juice from sound winter apples, pour the juice into moisture-vaporproof, liquid-tight containers, allowing 1 inch headspace, and freeze at once. The secret of really fresh-flavored golden apple juice is in the speed with which it is handled and put in the freezer. Fermentation starts almost immediately, and if the juice is allowed to remain at room temperature for even an hour, it begins to darken and develops a "cider" flavor.

Cherries, Grapes, and Berries must be heated to extract the juice. Select fully ripe, flavorful fruit. Wash, sort, and drain the fruit and put it in a stainless-steel or aluminum preserving kettle. Crush the fruit with a potato masher and heat it very gradually to between 160 and 170° F., stirring occasionally, to soften the fruit and release the juices. Strain the juice through a muslin jelly bag and cool by floating the saucepan containing it in ice water. Sweeten the juice with from ½ to 1 cup sugar per gallon of juice, or sweeten to taste. Pour the juice into moisture-vaporproof, liquid-tight containers, leaving 1 inch headspace for expansion during freezing, and freeze immediately.

Apricots, Peaches, and Rhubarb must also be heated to extract the juice, and since these are drier fruits than cherries or berries, a little water should be added. Wash, sort, and drain the fruit. Put it in a stainless-steel or aluminum kettle and add about ½ cup water for each pound of fruit.

Bring the fruit to a simmer, mashing it occasionally with a potato masher, and simmer very gently for 10 minutes. Strain the juice while it is hot through a jelly bag and cool the juice by floating the saucepan containing it in ice water. Sweeten the juice to taste, pour it into moisture-vaporproof, liquid-tight containers, leaving 1 inch headspace for expansion, and freeze immediately.

Tomatoes should be fully ripe and sound. Wash, core, and quarter, discarding any green portions. Heat the tomatoes slowly in a stainless-steel or aluminum kettle until the juice begins to boil and press juice and pulp through a fine sieve. Cool the juice over ice water and add 2 tablespoons of salt to each gallon of juice, or salt to taste. Other seasonings such as pepper and celery salt, or herbs such as fresh marjoram, garlic, or thyme, may also be added to taste. Pour the seasoned juice into moisture-vaporproof, liquid-tight containers and freeze immediately.

FRUIT PURÉES AND APPLESAUCE

Fruit purées, or "sieved" fruit pulp, are destined to become one of the most popular and flavorful products you can store in your home freezer because they retain their quality for long periods of frozen storage and they can be used in so many glamorous ways, in ice creams, sherbets, and other frozen desserts; in puddings, cake frostings, pie- and tart-shell fillings; in fillings for sweet rolls or breakfast rings; in whips, beverages, confections, and so on. A little purée may be cooked with sugar to make a small batch of fresh jam.

The purées are invaluable in dressing up any meal, as well as adding fruit to the daily diet. Already nearly a dozen different flavors of fruit purées are being produced commercially and whether you decide to make them yourself or depend on the reliable frozen-food packers is up to you, but everyone should have several of his favorite purées on hand in his freezer. The various flavors now on the market are apricot, banana, boysenberry, lemon, orange, tangerine, nectarine, peach, plum, raspberry, and strawberry. Other excellent purées—cherry, blackberry, cantaloupe, and the more exotic fruit like guavas and mangoes—may soon be commercially frozen.

Berries, peaches, plums, apricots, cherries, and grapes are some of the best fruits for purée, and the making and freezing of them takes little time.

Select fully ripe fruit of the finest flavor. Actually the fruit can be too mellow for canning and still produce the best flavor for a purée. It must, however, be perfectly good.

Wash and sort the fruit and trim away any blemishes or over-ripe spots. Mash the fruit pulp and deal with it in the same manner as if you were making fruit juice, except that instead of straining the juice through a sieve you must press both juice and pulp through a fine sieve, or put it through a food mill. Heat in a stainless-steel or aluminum kettle those fruits, such as cherries and plums and guavas, that need heating in order to start the juices flowing; soft fruits such as cantaloupe, papaya, persimmons, mangoes, and berries need nothing except mashing and being pressed through a sieve.

Mix the purée with a small amount of sugar to taste, cool over ice water, and package in moisture-vaporproof, liquid-tight containers, leaving ¾ inch headspace. Freeze immediately.

Strawberries. Select fully ripe strawberries of fine sweet flavor. Wash, drain, and stem them and press them through a fine sieve. Don't force through the very last of the pulp as this contains most of the seeds and is apt to give an off flavor to the purée. Five quarts of whole fresh fruit make about 6 cups of purée.

Other Berries. Wash and pick over the berries and press them through a fine sieve. Four quarts of whole fresh berries make about 6 cups of purée.

Cantaloupe. Peel and slice fully ripe cantaloupe, discarding the seeds, and press the flesh through a fine sieve. Six pounds of whole melons make about 6 cups of purée. Papayas, persimmons, and ripe mangoes may be puréed in the same way.

Cranberries. Wash and pick over the berries. Cook them in a little water in a tightly covered saucepan until the skins burst, and press both cranberries and the juice remaining in the pan through a fine sieve. Three quarts of whole fresh cranberries make about 6 cups of purée.

Concord Grapes. Wash and stem the grapes. Place them in a stainless-steel or aluminum kettle and crush them with a potato masher. Cover the kettle and bring the grapes to a simmer and heat until the juice begins to flow and the seeds are loosened from the pulp. Press through a fine sieve. Six pounds of fresh grapes make about 6 cups of purée. Cherries, plums, and guavas may be puréed in the same way.

Peaches, Apricots, and Nectarines. Select fully ripe, full-flavored fruit. Peel them, trim away any bruised spots, quarter, and discard the pits. Drop the fruit into boiling syrup made by dissolving 1 cup sugar in 8 cups water and simmer for 3 minutes. Press the fruit through a fine sieve and cool the purée over ice water. Six pounds of whole fruit make about 6 cups of purée.

Rhubarb. Wash the rhubarb and cut the stalks into 1-inch pieces. Heat in a saucepan placed over boiling water until the rhubarb is soft and press through a fine sieve. Cool the purée over ice water. Four pounds of cut rhubarb make about 6 cups of purée.

Packaging

Combine 6 cups fruit purée with from 1½ to 2 cups sugar, depending on the tartness of the fruit and personal taste. Stir the purée until the sugar is completely dissolved.

Package in moisture-vaporproof, liquid-tight containers, or in glass jars, leaving 1 inch headspace for expansion during freezing.

BLENDED FRUIT FOR YOUR FREEZER

If you are fortunate enough to have a mechanical blender, blended fruits have more flavor and nutritional qualities to offer you than fruit purées, because they usually contain both the skin and the pulp. They are strained only when it is necessary to remove the seeds.

Blueberry. Bring to a boil 1 pound of blueberries (about 3 cups) and ¼ cup water. Turn the berries and juice into the glass container of a blender, cover, and blend for about 1 minute, or until the mixture is smooth. Stir in ⅓ cup sugar and cool the blended fruit over the ice water. Package in moisture-vaporproof, liquid-tight containers and freeze. Makes 2½ cups.

Peach or Apricot. Blanch 1½ pounds of peaches for 1 minute in boiling water. Dip them into cold water, peel, halve, and pit. Bring to a boil 3 cups water and 1 cup sugar and cook the peach halves in the syrup for 3 minutes. Place the peaches in the glass container of a blender, cover, and blend for about 1 minute, or until the fruit is a smooth purée. Add ⅓ cup sugar and stir until the sugar is dissolved. Cool the blended fruit over ice water, package in moisture-vaporproof, liquid-tight containers, and freeze. Makes about 2⅔ cups.

Plum. Bring to a boil 1 pound halved, pitted ripe plums (about 2½ cups) and ¼ cup water and cook for 2 minutes. Turn the plums and their juice into the glass container of a blender, cover, and blend for about 1 minute, or until the plums are smooth. Add

¼ cup sugar and stir until the sugar is dissolved. Cool the blended fruit over ice water, package in moisture-vaporproof, liquid-tight containers, and freeze. Makes about 2½ cups.

Rhubarb. Bring to a boil 1 pound cut rhubarb stalks (about 3 cups) and ½ cup water, cover, and cook for 2 minutes. Turn the rhubarb and the juice into the glass container of a blender, cover, and blend for about 1 minute, or until the rhubarb is smooth. Stir in ½ cup sugar and stir until the sugar is dissolved. Cook the blended fruit over ice water, package in moisture-vaporproof, liquid-tight containers, and freeze. Makes about 2⅔ cups.

Strawberry. Wash and hull 1 pound strawberries (about 3½ cups). Put them in the glass container of a blender and add 2 tablespoons water. Cover and blend for about 1 minute, or until the fruit is smooth. Stir in ⅓ cup sugar and cool the blended strawberries over ice water. Package in moisture-vaporproof, liquid-tight containers and freeze. Makes about 2½ cups.

Tomato. Wash 2 pounds tomatoes and cut them into quarters, discarding any green or overripe spots. Bring them to a boil, cook for 3 minutes, and drain lightly. Put the tomatoes in the glass container of a blender, cover, and blend for about 10 seconds, or until smooth. Strain the blended tomatoes, stir in 1¼ teaspoons salt, or salt and other seasonings to taste, and cool over ice water. Pack the blended tomatoes into moisture-vaporproof, liquid-tight containers and freeze. Makes 2⅔ cups.

Velva fruit

"Velva fruit" is the name given to a fruit purée mixed with sugar to sweeten it, and gelatin to make it smooth as velvet, by the Western Regional Laboratory of the Bureau of Agricultural and Industrial Chemistry, which was working with the original discoverers, the Bureau of Human Nutrition and Home Economics.

Velva fruit may be made and stored in your home freezer for a deliciously cool and flavorful dessert at any time, or it may be made from the frozen fruit purée.

To use the frozen purée, put the sealed container in cold or lukewarm water to speed the thawing. A quart of purée will thaw in about 2 hours. When the purée reaches room temperature, proceed as if you were using the freshly made fruit purée.

VELVA FRUIT RECIPE
>   6 cups fresh or frozen and defrosted fruit purée
>   1½ to 2 cups sugar, if fresh purée is used
>   2 tablespoons lemon juice, or to taste
>   ½ teaspoon salt
>   2 tablespoons gelatin
>   ½ cup water

Combine fresh fruit purée and sugar, lemon juice, and salt. Or combine frozen thawed fruit purée with only the lemon juice and salt. Soak the gelatin in the water for 5 minutes and dissolve it by heating it over hot water for 10 minutes. Add the flavored purée slowly to the gelatin, stirring continuously and vigorously. Freeze the mixture in an ice-cream freezer for the most enjoyable eating, or freeze it in the tray of your refrigerator. It will be good, but not as good as if it were made in the old-fashioned way.

TO FREEZE IN THE REFRIGERATOR

Place the fruit mixture in a deep refrigerator tray, turn the temperature control to the coldest point, and freeze until the fruit is firm. Turn it into a chilled bowl and beat it with a wooden spoon, or an electric mixer, until the mixture becomes smooth in texture and increases in volume. Return Velva fruit to the refrigerator tray and freeze for a few hours, or until it is firm again. Makes 1 gallon.

Serve for dinner, or pack in moisture-vaporproof cartons and store for not more than 2 weeks.

HOW TO USE FROZEN FRUITS

Frozen fruits are ready to be served as soon as they are thawed and if the fruit was carefully selected and prepared for your freezer, the flavor is almost the same as that of fresh fruit.

Always thaw fruit in the sealed container in which it was frozen to preserve the best color and turn the container several times during the thawing to keep the fruit bathed in the juice. On the refrigerator shelf a 1-pound package of fruit will thaw in 6 to 8 hours. At room temperature it will defrost in 2 to 3 hours. To thaw fruit quickly, place the package in cool running water for 30 minutes. Fruit packed with dry sugar will thaw a little more quickly than that packed with syrup.

Frozen fruit loses texture and flavor very quickly after it is thawed. So it is best to cook any leftover frozen and defrosted fruit and serve it in a compote, pudding, or other cooked dessert.

Serve berries while they still contain a few ice crystals. And the texture of peaches and most other fruits is better when they are served very cold. On the other hand, the flavor is improved by more complete thawing.

Most frozen fruits may be used in the same way as fresh fruit. They make excellent desserts served alone, or combined with ice cream. Or they may be used in pies, shortcakes, puddings, muffins, cobblers, upside-down cakes, or made into jams, jellies, and preserves.

Pies and tarts

For a 9-inch pie, or for 8 tarts, thaw 1 quart of frozen fruit only long enough to be able to separate the pieces. If the fruit was packed without sugar, add the amount of sugar called for in the recipe you are using. If the fruit was packed with dry sugar in the proportion of 4 parts fruit to 1 part sugar, no sugar at all should be added. If the fruit was packed in syrup, drain off the syrup, measure ½ cup, and add it to the quart of fruit in the pie. Reserve the remaining syrup to use in fruit drinks, compotes, or fruit sauces.

Frozen fruits develop more juice than fresh, so add a little more thickening to pies and tarts made with the frozen product.

Muffins and pancakes

Thaw frozen berries or other fruit just long enough to be able to separate the pieces and add to the flour mixture before stirring in the liquid.

Upside-down cake

Thaw frozen fruit in its container just long enough to be able to separate the pieces and arrange it in a buttered baking dish. Prepare a cake batter according to your favorite recipe, pour it over the fruit, and bake.

Jellies, jams, and preserves

Whole fruit, fruit juices, or purées need not be defrosted, but may be emptied directly into the cooking utensil. Follow a good recipe and make allowance for the sugar added to the fruit before it was frozen.

Details of home-freezing fruits

APPLES FOR PIE

Suggested varieties: Any high-acid variety
1 bushel (48 pounds) yields 20–22 quarts

Since winter apples keep beautifully if carefully stored in a cold room, there is little point in filling up the freezer with them, unless there happens to be a real shortage and you and your family just can't get along without apple pie.

Select only firm-ripe sour apples in prime condition for eating.
Peel, core, and cut apples into slices for pie. Small apples should be sliced into eighths and large ones into twelfths. Peel only a few

apples at one time, as the cut surfaces of apples discolor rapidly on exposure to the air. The browning may be prevented in either of two ways:

1. Drop the apple slices directly into a solution made by dissolving 3 teaspoons salt in 2 quarts cold water, or 3 tablespoons lemon juice or 2 tablespoons citric acid dissolved in 2 quarts cold water. Remove the apples from the solution after 1 minute and drain. Then scald the slices in steam for 90 seconds and cool them in ice water.

2. Submerge the apple slices for 5 minutes in a solution made by dissolving 1½ teaspoons sodium sulphite in 1 gallon of cold water. Be sure to mix the solution in an earthenware, glass, stainless-steel, or enameled container.

Drain the apple slices on absorbent paper.

Package without sugar, or sugar may be added in the proportion of 1 pound sugar to 4 pounds fruit.

Seal and freeze immediately.

A quart of apple slices makes a 9-inch pie.

APPLESAUCE

> *Suggested varieties:*   Baldwin
>   Greening
>   Northern Spy
>   Yellow Transparent

   1 bushel (48 pounds) yields 23–25 quarts

Either winter or summer apples may be used to make delicious applesauce, but since winter apples can be stored, it is a good idea to make sauce from summer apples.

Select fine-flavored apples.

Stem the apples, cut away any bruises or bad spots, and cut them into eighths. Put them in a saucepan with only enough water to prevent the apples from sticking to the bottom of the pan and bring to a fast boil. Reduce the heat and simmer for about 10 minutes, or until the apples are mushy. Force the apple pulp through a sieve and stir in sugar to taste.

Cool the applesauce over ice water, package, and freeze promptly.

Apple compote

Peel, core, and slice apples and stew them in sugar syrup in the usual way. A stick of cinnamon may be added, or any other favorite spice. Cool the stewed apples, package with the syrup, and freeze.

Baked apples

Bake apples according to your favorite recipe, filling the centers with raisins or nuts, brown sugar, butter, and spice. Cool them over ice water and wrap individually in freezer paper. Package as many as you will need for one meal in a carton, seal, and freeze. Defrost in a moderate oven (350° F.) for 30 minutes, basting them occasionally with a little melted butter and sherry or rum.

APRICOTS

Suggested varieties: Tilton
Royal
Blenheim
Moorpark

1 crate (16 pounds) yields 10 quarts

Select tree-ripened fruit, brightly colored, richly flavored, with no trace of green and with easily removable pits.

Wash the apricots thoroughly and remove the stems. Plunge about 12 apricots at a time in boiling water for 30 seconds to loosen the skins. Remove and plunge them into ice water to cover for 1 minute. Peel the apricots, cut them into halves, and remove the pits.

Pack the apricot halves in containers and cover them with a 50% syrup to which has been added ¼ teaspoon ascorbic acid to each cup of syrup (see Index). Place a crumpled piece of freezer paper on the fruit under the top of the container to keep them submerged in the syrup.

Seal and freeze at once.

AVOCADOS (purée only)

Select avocados that are just ready to be eaten. They should not be hard or mushy. The small dark-skinned Calavos have a nuttier and better flavor.

Wash the avocados, cut them in half, and remove the pits. Scoop the pulp from the rind and mash the pulp with 2 teaspoons lemon or lime juice and 1½ teaspoons sugar for each avocado. Refill the shell with the purée, wrap individually in moisture-vaporproof paper, and freeze immediately.

Avocados prepared in this way are delicious served for dessert and very colorful too if a fluted border of whipped cream is piped all around near the shell. Sprinkle the center with finely chopped pistachio nuts.

Do not store longer than 1 month.

The velvety smooth texture of avocado purée lends itself to creamy frozen desserts, ices, and ice creams. The avocado gives a delicate nutty taste to the ice cream, blends well with other fruit flavors, and because of the large amount of oil in the pulp, adds richness to the cream.

Avocado-pineapple ice

2 cups pineapple juice
¾ cup sugar
½ cup lemon juice
Pinch of salt
1 ripe avocado

Combine the pineapple juice and sugar, heat to just below the boiling point, and cool. Stir in the lemon juice and salt. Pour the mixture into a refrigerator tray and freeze to a mush. Cut the avocado in half, peel, and remove the seed. Mash the fruit to a pulp and beat it into the frozen mixture. Return to the freezing compartment and freeze until firm. Serve for dinner, or pack in moisture-vaporproof cartons and store for not more than 2 weeks.

BERRIES
(blackberries, boysenberries, dewberries, loganberries, youngberries, and nectarberries)

A 24-quart crate (36 pounds) yields 24–26 quarts

Blackberries, dewberries, and boysenberries are probably the least desirable of all frozen fruits.

Select firm, sweet, plump, fully ripened berries with fine flavor. If the berries are from your own garden crop, do not pick them after a heavy rain, or during extremely hot weather.

Pick over the berries and discard any that are bruised, underripe, poorly colored, badly formed, or overseedy. Wash a few at a time in ice water and drain them in a colander, or on absorbent paper.

Syrup pack. Place the berries in moisture-vaporproof, liquid-tight containers and cover them with a 40 or 50% syrup, leaving ¾ inch headspace. Berries packed in syrup are good for a dessert sauce or an ice-cream topping.

Sugar pack. Sprinkle 4 pounds berries with 1 pound sugar and mix lightly with a wooden spoon until the fruit is coated with the sugar. Use for pies or in the making of preserves.

Package and freeze immediately.

A quart of berries makes a 9-inch pie.

BLUEBERRIES

Suggested varieties: Concord
                          Pioneer
                          Wild Low Bush

A 24-quart crate (36 pounds) yields 24–26 quarts

Select large, tender-skinned blueberries with a sweet flavor.

Wash the blueberries thoroughly and discard the leaves and berries that are immature or shriveled and drain.

Dry pack. This is the best method if the blueberries are to be used in pies, muffins, or pancakes.

Sugar pack. Place blueberries in a dish, sprinkle them with sugar in the proportion of 5 parts berries to 1 part sugar, and mix well, crushing them slightly. For use in blueberry shortcake, as a fruit sauce, in ice creams and frozen desserts, or as an ice-cream topping.

Package, seal, and freeze.

CANTALOUPE (also papaya)

6 large cantaloupe yield 10 quarts

Select firm-fleshed but well ripened melons with fine flavor. The deep yellow varieties are best.

Cut the melons in half and discard the seeds. Scoop out the flesh with a French potato-ball cutter, or peel the melons and cut the flesh into uniform slices or cubes. Drain well.

Dry pack the melon balls, slices, or cubes in layers, separating each layer with two pieces of freezer paper, so that the pieces may be easily separated for serving, before they are completely thawed, in fruit cups or salads.

Package in moisture-vaporproof containers, seal, and freeze.

CHERRIES, SOUR

Suggested varieties: Montmorency
                         English Morello

1 bushel (56 pounds) yields 18 quarts

Select tender-skinned, bright-red cherries with a characteristic tart flavor.
Wash the cherries in ice water, stem, and pit.

Sugar pack. Mix 1 pound sugar with 4 pounds cherries.
Package in moisture-vaporproof, liquid-tight containers, seal, and freeze promptly.
Frozen sour cherries are delicious made into pies and cobblers. Frozen-cherry juice is excellent in punches and sherbets.

CHERRIES, SWEET

Suggested varieties: Lambert
                         Bing

1 bushel (56 pounds) yields 19 quarts

Select firm, fully ripe, tree-ripened berries with rich flavor.
Wash the cherries in ice water, stem, and pit if desired, depending on how you wish to serve them.

Syrup pack. Whether pitted or whole, cherries should be packed in a 40 or 50% syrup to which is added ¼ teaspoon ascorbic acid to each cup of syrup. Sweet cherries are excellent for an ice-cream sauce, if slightly crushed, or for Cherries Jubilee.
Package in moisture-vaporproof, liquid-tight containers, seal, and freeze immediately.

COCONUT

Unsweetened coconut, grated and mixed with its own milk, makes an excellent frozen product for use in curry sauces, desserts, cake frostings, or ice creams.

Or 1 part sugar may be added to every 8 parts shredded coconut. Stir in the coconut milk for extra flavor.

Package in moisture-vaporproof, liquid-tight containers, seal, and freeze.

CRANBERRIES

Suggested varieties: Howes
Early Black

1 pound yields 1 quart

Select deep red, glossy skinned cranberries with a mealy texture.

Wash and sort the cranberries and discard any that are soft or poorly formed. Drain.

Dry pack. Cranberries need no sugar or syrup. They are packed with nothing added, available at any time to make into sauce or jelly, or they may be made into a sauce by your favorite recipe and the sauce frozen in advance for holiday meals.

Dry-packed cranberries may be packed in moisture-vaporproof, heat-sealing bags, but the sauce must be packaged in liquid-tight containers.

Seal and freeze.

CURRANTS

Any large variety is good for freezing
2 quarts (3 pounds) yield 2 quarts

Select bright-red, well-ripened berries.

Stem the currants, wash, and drain.

Dry pack is good for jelly making later in the season, when you might like to combine them with apple or raspberry juice.

Sugar pack for use in pies, tarts, and cobblers. Crush the currants lightly and mix 3 parts fruit with 1 part sugar.

Package, seal, and freeze.

FIGS

> *Suggested varieties:*   Magnolia
>   Brown Turkey
>   Celestial
>   Kadota
>   Mission

Select figs with tender skins and flesh that is soft.

Wash the figs carefully and discard any that are split or show signs of internal rot or souring.

Figs may be peeled, if desired, halved, sliced, or left whole.

Syrup pack. Cover the figs with a 40 to 50% syrup.

Package according to family needs in moisture-vaporproof, liquid-tight containers, allowing 3 or 4 figs per serving.

Seal and freeze immediately.

GOOSEBERRIES

> *Any large variety freezes well*
> 4 quarts yield 7 pints

Select fully matured, ripe berries with just a little red color.

Wash the gooseberries in cold water, drain, and remove the stems and blossom ends.

Sugar pack. Mix the gooseberries with 1 part sugar to 3 parts berries.

Package, seal, and freeze.

GRAPEFRUIT AND ORANGE SECTIONS

All varieties of oranges freeze well. Select them for their fine flavor.

Thin-skinned grapefruit that section easily are preferable, but again it is better to select grapefruit for flavor and sweetness.

Chill the fruit in the refrigerator. Peel them, removing all the white skin, and cut the sections free from the membranes. Discard the seeds.

Package in layers with two sheets of freezer paper between the layers so the sections may be separated, while still partially frozen, for use in fruit cups and salads. Grapefruit sections may be sprinkled with sugar to taste, if you wish.

Orange and grapefruit sections may also be packaged in combination with other fruits, such as cantaloupe, grapes, papaya, unpitted cherries, watermelon, and pineapple.

GRAPES

Select firm, ripe table grapes with tender skins and sweet flavor. Wash, sort, discard any soft or shriveled grapes, and drain.

Dry pack or *syrup pack*. Cover with 40% syrup for use in fruit cocktails and salads.

Concord grapes for pie

Separate the pulp and hulls. Simmer the pulp for 5 minutes, press through a fine sieve, and discard the seeds. Simmer the hulls for 20 minutes to soften them, combine puréed pulp and hulls, and stir in 1 part sugar to 3 parts by weight of the combined pulp and hulls.

Package in moisture-vaporproof, liquid-tight containers in quart size, which is sufficient for a 9-inch pie.

HUCKLEBERRIES. See BLUEBERRIES

PEACHES (also nectarines)

Suggested varieties: Yellow-Hale Haven
J. H. Hale
South Haven
White-Golden Jubilee
Georgia Belle

1 bushel (48 pounds) yields 24 quarts

White peaches do not make as good frozen products as the yellow varieties.

Select peaches that are just right for eating. They should be juicy, tree-ripened fruit with firm, fine-grained flesh. The free-stone types with red-colored pit cavities make the most attractive frozen product.

Place 12 peaches in a wire basket and plunge them into boiling water to cover for 30 seconds, then plunge them into ice water and peel. Slice the peaches directly into cold syrup in moisture-vapor-proof, liquid-tight containers. The syrup should be made in advance by dissolving 3 cups sugar in each 4 cups water. Chill the syrup and when ready to use, gently stir 1 teaspoon ascorbic acid into each quart of the syrup.

Press the fruit down in the container and add enough cold syrup to cover it, leaving ½ inch headspace in pints and 1 inch in quarts. Place a crumpled piece of freezer paper on top of the fruit, under the container top, to hold the fruit under the syrup.

Seal and freeze.

Frozen peaches make delicious pies, shortcakes, and upside-down cakes. They may be served as fresh fruit or as an ice-cream topping when only partially thawed.

Peaches and nectarines that are crushed or puréed without first being poached in syrup should also be mixed with ascorbic acid (½ teaspoon per pint of purée) to retain the color during frozen storage. Stir the ascorbic acid into the purée with 1 part sugar to 3 parts purée. Stir gently until the sugar is dissolved, being careful not to whip in any air. Delicious for ice creams, mousses, soufflés, and filling for tiny thin pancakes.

PEARS

> *Suggested varieties:*   Kieffer
> Baldwin
>
> 2 dozen (8 pounds) yield 4 quarts

Select tender, juicy, fine-fleshed pears.

Peel, halve, and core the pears. Slice them lengthwise about ½ inch thick directly into cold syrup in moisture-vaporproof, liquid-tight containers. The syrup should be from 40 to 50%, and it should contain ¼ teaspoon ascorbic acid per cup.

Or the sliced pears should be immersed in boiling syrup for 2 minutes, then packed in the containers and covered with cold syrup, leaving ½ inch headspace in pints and 1 inch headspace in quarts. Place a crumpled piece of freezer paper over the fruit, under the lid of the container, to keep the fruit covered with the syrup.

Seal and freeze.

After thawing, pears can be used in pies, cobblers, fruit cocktail, or salads.

PINEAPPLE

> *Any standard market pineapple is good for freezing.*
> 1 pineapple (3 pounds) yields 3 pint cartons or 12 to 14 slices

Select ripe pineapple with a fragrant odor and sweet flavor.

Cut the pineapple into slices ¾ inch thick, remove the outer skin and the eyes from each slice, and cut out the core.

The pineapple slices need neither sugar nor syrup, and they may be frozen whole in rigid tubs or containers with 2 pieces of freezer paper between slices so they may be separated easily while still frozen. Or they may be stacked on moisture-vaporproof paper with two layers of freezer paper between layers and the re-formed pineapple wrapped carefully in the paper.

Shredded pineapple or cubes may be packed in a light syrup for use in dessert sauces.

PLUMS AND PRUNES

> *Suggested varieties:*   Damson
> Red June
> Italian Prune

> 1 crate (20 pounds) yields 8 quarts

Select fully ripened plums.

Wash and sort the plums. Discard any that are bruised or damaged, immature, or overripe. Cut the plums in half, remove the pits, and drop them directly into moisture-vaporproof, liquid-tight containers containing a 40 to 50% syrup with ¼ teaspoon ascorbic acid added to each cup.

Seal and freeze.

RASPBERRIES, RED

> *Suggested varieties:*   Cuthbert
> Latham
> Viking

> A 24-quart crate (36 pounds) yields 24 to 26 quarts

Select large, ripe berries.

Raspberries are exceptionally fragile and care must be taken in handling them or they will bruise. Wash only a few at a time in ice water and drain them on absorbent paper.

Sugar pack. Pack berries directly into moisture-vaporproof, liquid-tight containers. Use 1 cup sugar to 4 cups berries. When the container is ¼ full, add ¼ of the sugar and continue to alternate layers of berries and sugar until the container is full. Raspberries will make their own syrup when sugar is added.

Seal and freeze promptly.

RHUBARB

Suggested variety: Victoria

15 pounds yield 11 quarts

Select tender, deep red-colored stalks early in the spring before the rhubarb has become tough.

Wash rhubarb well under running water and cut the stalks into 1-inch pieces.

Dry pack. Rhubarb does not need sugar or sugar syrup. Simply pack it in moisture-vaporproof cartons or bags.

Sugar pack. Rhubarb may be packed with 1 part by weight of sugar to every 4 or 5 parts by weight of rhubarb. Use liquid-tight containers.

Seal and freeze.

Rhubarb may also be stewed or steamed according to your favorite method, sweetened to taste, and frozen. Pack it in moisture-vaporproof, liquid-tight containers leaving ½ inch headspace. Seal and freeze.

STRAWBERRIES

Suggested varieties: Marshall
Redheart
Beaver
Dunlap
Catskill

A 24-quart crate (36 pounds) yields 30 quarts

Select ripe-all-over, sound, firm berries with slightly tart flavor. Wash the berries, a few at a time, in ice water, drain them, and remove the hulls.

Strawberries may be frozen whole in sugar syrup, or as a purée or juice, but for the fullest, finest flavor, strawberries should be sliced or crushed and mixed with dry sugar.

Sugar pack. Slice the strawberries into a bowl and crush them lightly if desired. Sprinkle them with 1 cup sugar to 4 cups fruit and toss with a wooden spoon until the berries are coated with sugar.

Syrup pack. Whole strawberries hold shape better if they are packed in 40% sugar syrup, as this method is less likely to bruise the delicate fruit. The flavor of whole strawberries packed in syrup is not so good, however, as the sliced sugar-packed berries. The syrup contains water which dilutes the strawberry flavor.

Pack berries in moisture-vaporproof, liquid-tight containers, leaving ½ inch headspace in pint containers and 1 inch headspace in quarts. Place a crumpled piece of freezer paper on top of the berries under the container lid to keep them immersed in the syrup.

Seal and freeze.

WATERMELON

Any thoroughly ripened watermelon is excellent for freezing for fruit cups or fruit salads, but the red-ripe center of the watermelon is best. Prepare and freeze watermelon according to the directions for cantaloupe.

CHAPTER SEVEN

How to freeze eggs and dairy products

EGGS

Eggs freeze perfectly—in fact, you cannot tell frozen eggs from fresh after as long as 6 to 8 months' storage. Naturally, we take for granted that they are strictly fresh before they are frozen, for, once again, the frozen product is only as good as the original.

Eggs are usually scarce from November through March. When they are plentiful and reasonable in price, however, they are a most economical product to store in your freezer.

Don't freeze large quantities of eggs in one container unless you know that the amount will be entirely used when it is removed from the freezer. Package eggs in amounts needed for specific recipes and cooking uses. You are well aware of your family's favorite dishes requiring eggs, so you will want to be prepared to take from your freezer just 3 whole eggs for that special chocolate cake, 5 egg yolks for a custard or a sponge cake, 8 egg whites for an angel food. If you are fond of cream puffs, you will want several packages of 4 whole eggs, and so on.

Eggs cannot be frozen in their shells, as the expansion during freezing would crack them. After being removed from the shells, they may be frozen whole or separated into yolks and whites.

Whole eggs and egg yolks must be lightly beaten and mixed with a small amount of salt or sugar. The amount needed is so small that it is not noticeable in the cooked product. Still, you may wish to designate the sweetened eggs for use in baked products and the salted ones for omelettes, mayonnaise, et cetera. But the amount of salt added would be imperceptible in any dish and most baked products and sweet dishes of all kinds are improved by the touch of salt. Should a recipe call for a pinch of salt, you may simply eliminate it from the ingredients when using frozen salted eggs.

WHOLE EGGS

Wash the egg shells and break each egg into a cup before combining in a bowl, so it can be discarded if it is not strictly fresh. Beat the eggs with a fork, or a rotary beater, just long enough to combine thoroughly the yolks and the whites, but without beating air into them. Stir in 1 teaspoon salt or 1 tablespoon sugar or corn syrup for each 2 cups of mixed whole eggs. It will take about 5 whole eggs to make 1 cup.

SEPARATED EGGS

Wash the egg shells, break each egg carefully, and separate the yolk from the white. Remember that even a speck of the fat egg yolk left in the whites will prevent them from being beaten into a thick, staple foam. Should a speck of yolk fall into the whites, lift it out with the sharp edge of a broken egg shell.

Beat the egg yolks lightly with a fork, or rotary beater, until they are thoroughly mixed, but be careful not to beat air into them. Stir in 1 teaspoon salt or 1 tablespoon sugar or corn syrup to each cup of yolks. It will take about 14 yolks to make 1 cup. Strain the egg yolks through a fine sieve and skim off any air bubbles from the surface before freezing to prevent a crust from forming.

Egg whites do not coagulate when they are frozen and they need no mixing nor any addition of salt or sugar. Simply pour them into a container, label, and freeze. It will take about 8 egg whites to make 1 cup. When they are thawed, they beat to a volume that is equal to that of the fresh product.

How to package eggs for the freezer

Eggs may be frozen in small Cellophane bags, each bag containing the number of eggs for a specific use, and several bags may be

packed into a carton. Or the eggs may be frozen in leakproof wax-
lined cartons, leaving ½ inch headspace for expansion. But the
neatest trick of the year, and I don't know who dreamed it up or I
would give credit here, is to freeze eggs in plastic ice cube trays.
One whole egg, mixed white and yolk, or 2 egg whites, or 2 or 3
mixed egg yolks, can be frozen in each cube. Once frozen, they can
be taken from the tray and packaged in a long, thin bag of heat-
sealing moisture-vaporproof material. Use a lukewarm curling iron
and seal directly across the bag, separating each frozen egg cube. In
this way, a cube or two, depending on how much you need, may be
snipped off with a pair of scissors and the bag returned to the
freezer.

LABEL CLEARLY
    Label each package of eggs with the amount, whether mixed with
salt or sugar, the date, and proposed use: EGG WHITES, 1 CUP FOR
ANGEL FOOD; 4 EGG YOLKS WITH SUGAR FOR CUSTARD, et cetera.

Using frozen eggs

    Let the eggs thaw in the unopened package in the refrigerator or
at room temperature. Small amounts of eggs packaged for specific
cooking purposes will thaw in 30 minutes at room temperature. In
an emergency, eggs packed in watertight packages may be defrosted
quickly in a bowl of lukewarm water.
    Use defrosted whole mixed eggs and yolks promptly. Egg whites
will remain fresh in the refrigerator for several days.
    Use whole eggs in omelettes, scrambled eggs, custards, ice cream,
cakes, breads, pancakes, fritters, waffles, croquettes, and cream
puffs.
    Use egg yolks in sponge cakes, custards, sauces, and mayonnaise.
    Use egg whites in meringues, icings, angel food and other white
cakes, candies, cookies, sherbets, and desserts.

AMOUNTS EQUIVALENT TO 1 FRESH EGG:
    2½ tablespoons mixed whites and yolks
    1½ tablespoons whites
    1 tablespoon yolks

BUTTER

Butter will keep fresh and sweet for many months in your freezer providing it is made from freshly pasteurized sweet cream. Butter made from unpasteurized sweet cream does not retain its quality as long and that made from unpasteurized sour cream may become rancid in a few weeks. Sweet butter will keep for a year. Salted butter should not be stored for longer than 6 months, since the salt speeds up the development of rancidity in any fat.

Cream may be pasteurized by heating it to 145° F. and holding it there for 30 minutes. Cool the cream quickly to 50° F. and let it stand for 3 hours before churning. After churning, work it well to remove the buttermilk.

Pack butter in heavily waxed cartons, or wrap it in moisture-vaporproof paper. Commercial butter should be left in its original carton and overwrapped with moisture-vaporproof paper.

CHEESE

Cheeses of all kinds, with the one exception of cream cheese, freeze well, and may be kept from 4 to 6 months in the freezer. The quality of soft cheeses that are purchased at the exact degree of ripeness to suit your palate will retain this perfect stage and the flavor and texture are not affected. Blue cheese or Roquefort that have been frozen are apt to be more crumbly than fresh.

Cut cheese into family-sized portions and wrap in moisture-vaporproof paper so that the cheese will not dry out or transfer its flavor to other foods.

Cottage cheese

Cottage cheese uncreamed and of good quality will keep well in the freezer for 3 to 4 months. Package it firmly in moisture-vaporproof cartons, pressing out as much air as possible and leaving ½ inch headspace for expansion. Thaw in the refrigerator and add cream, if desired, at the time of serving.

CREAM

Cream separates during freezing and is not suitable for table use, nor does frozen cream whip as well as fresh. There seems little reason for the city dweller to freeze cream, as heavy cream is readily available and, if left in its sterile container, will keep fresh in the average refrigerator for at least a week. Those who live on a farm may have good reason to freeze their surplus.

Cream to be frozen should contain from 40 to 60 per cent butterfat and the more butterfat it contains the better it will freeze. After separating, cream should be pasteurized within an hour at 145° F. for 30 minutes. It should be cooled quickly to 50° F. or lower, packed in liquid-tight, moisture-vaporproof containers—allowing 1 inch headspace for expansion during freezing—and frozen promptly. Cream should not be stored longer than 4 months and is best used in pastry creams and custards.

Frozen cream should be defrosted slowly in the refrigerator, in its original container.

ICE CREAM

Both homemade or commercially made ice cream and sherbet can be stored in the home freezer for several months to make quick and nourishing desserts. High-quality ice creams made from pasteurized cream and milk retain their flavor for 2 months. Those made from high-fat-content cream remain smooth in texture longer than those made from light cream or milk.

Commercially made ice cream and sherbet can be stored in the original container and overwrapped with moisture-vaporproof paper, or may be purchased in bulk and repacked in smaller moisture-vaporproof containers.

Chocolate-coated ice cream on sticks makes a quick and amusing

dessert for grownups as well as children, and can be eaten directly
from the freezer.

Homemade ice cream is the perfect way to use up a supply of
cream, rather than freezing the surplus supply of cream itself. Use
a recipe calling for a large percentage of heavy cream and a stabi-
lizer such as egg yolks or gelatin. Make it in a hand- or electrically-
turned ice cream freezer so that it will not become grainy during
storage. Several excellent recipes for ice cream are given in the last
chapter.

Ice cream molded into colorful shapes and *bombes* can add that
special touch to special occasions. Ice cream molds in the shape of
hearts, bells, shamrocks, Easter bunnies, Christmas trees, and many
others can be purchased from your local dairy, wrapped, and stored
in your freezer for holiday parties. Or you may be able to find molds
in a variety of shapes and freeze your own. Parfait and *bombe*
molds are available in better house-goods stores across the country.
And a little imagination will go a long way. Those silver-foil
Christmas bells used for decoration may be packed full of ice cream
and frozen. The foil can then be torn away from the ice cream bell,
and the ice cream wrapped and stored for future use.

Ice cream or ice cream combined with cake make many a cool-
some, ready-to-serve dessert. Here are a few:

Easter egg nests

Cut the center out of chocolate cup cakes to form nests. Brush
the edges of the nests with syrup and sprinkle them with shredded
coconut. Use a melon-ball scoop to fill the nest with little balls of
differently colored ice cream. Wrap each nest separately and freeze.
The nests may be stored for 1 month. Serve directly from the
freezer.

Coconut balls

Shape ice cream into balls with an ice cream scoop. Roll each
ball in shredded coconut, package individually, and freeze. Serve
directly from the freezer with chocolate, butterscotch, or fruit sauce.

Coconut balls may be stored for 2 months. One quart of ice cream will make 8 balls.

Snow men

With an ice cream scoop, form a large ball of ice cream. Make a smaller ball with a smaller ice cream scoop and place it on top of the large ball. With a toothpick dipped in melted chocolate, draw eyes, nose, and mouth on the flat side of a marshmallow. Fasten the marshmallow atop the small ball of ice cream with a toothpick and balance a red or green maraschino cherry on the marshmallow. Secure it with another toothpick. Stick currants down the front for buttons. Wrap each snow man in moisture-vaporproof paper and store in the freezer for as long as 1 month. Serve directly from the freezer. One quart of ice cream makes 4 snow men.

Ice cream cake roll

Spread a large sheet of golden or chocolate sponge cake with ice cream and roll it up lengthwise like a jelly roll. Frost the roll with butter cream icing and freeze. Wrap, and store for as long as 2 months. Serve directly from the freezer.

Strawberry ice cream roll

Spread a large sheet of sponge cake with 1 quart vanilla ice cream mixed with 1½ cups sliced fresh strawberries. Roll the cake up lengthwise like a jelly roll and frost it with heavy cream whipped and flavored with sugar and vanilla to taste. Place the roll in the freezer until the whipped cream is hard. Wrap and store in the freezer for as long as 2 months. Serve directly from the freezer.

Ice cream ribbon cake

Bake angel food in a loaf pan 10 × 5 × 3 inches and when it is cool cut it lengthwise into 3 layers. Spread a layer of ice cream 1

inch thick between the first and second layers of cake and ice cream
of another flavor and color between the second and top layers of
cake. Frost the top and sides with heavy cream whipped and flavored to taste, sprinkle with shredded coconut, and place in the
freezer until the whipped cream is hard. Wrap and store until ready
to serve directly from the freezer. It may be stored for 1 month.

Ice cream pie

Roll chocolate or vanilla wafers into fine crumbs and combine
2 cups of the crumbs with ¼ cup sugar and ½ cup softened butter.
Press the mixture over the bottom and sides of a buttered 9-inch pie
plate. Fill the shell with 1 quart of vanilla ice cream. Arrange sliced
and sugared fresh fruit, or partially thawed frozen fruit, on the ice
cream. Wrap and freeze. Will keep beautifully for 2 months. Serve
directly from the freezer.

Colettes

Melt a package of chocolate bits over a gentle heat with 2 tablespoons butter, stirring constantly. Brush a thin coating of the melted
chocolate on the bottom and sides of 8 small paper baking cups with
fluted edges. Chill the cups until the chocolate is set, then fill the
colettes with scoops of ice cream. Wrap individually and freeze. The
colettes will keep well for 2 months. Serve directly from the freezer.

Ice cream sandwiches

Cut a brick of ice cream into thin slices and put 2 slices together
with a layer of crushed fruit or berries between. Wrap each sandwich separately and freeze. Will keep well for 2 months. Serve directly from the freezer.

CHAPTER EIGHT

How to freeze bakery products, sandwiches, and canapés

Since the discovery that frozen bread is as fresh as freshly baked bread, that frozen pie dough is flakier than unfrozen, and that cakes and cookies remain fresh and retain their homemade quality for months, a wide variety of home-baked products on hand is rapidly becoming one of the most popular and efficient uses for the home freezer.

It is practical to make a sizable batch of bread dough for loaves and rolls, instead of a small quantity. It's economical to make 2 or 3 cakes, or 3 or 4 pies, while the oven is hot. Double or triple the quantity of any pastry or cake recipe can be made as quickly as the single recipe, and no more utensils need be washed!

Time is saved, your baking chores for a week or more are finished in a single afternoon, and your family will enjoy the flavor and the goodness of home-baked products.

BREAD AND ROLLS

Baked yeast breads

Yeast bread and rolls, baked before freezing, will remain fresh in your freezer for 6 months. Cool breads to room temperature after baking them, then wrap and seal in moisture-vaporproof material and freeze. Frozen loaves may be sliced while they are still frozen, or the amount needed for a meal can be cut from the loaf and the rest returned to the freezer.

Cool baked rolls to room temperature and package them in amounts sufficient for one meal. A variety of shapes and flavors—cloverleaf, parkerhouse, cinnamon, and so on—frozen together in one package make an attractive variety.

A good-sized batch of sweet yeast dough can be made into a wide selection of breakfast breads, tea rolls, buns, and sweet yeast cakes. Swedish coffee rings, *Küchen,* and stollens add variety to daily meals. They can be easily and quickly thawed by heating them in the oven, and served hot. Before they are packaged for the freezer, they must all be cooled to room temperature.

Baked breads thaw quickly at room temperature, because of their low moisture content. But the best way to serve them is hot. Heat them in a moderate oven (350° F.) for 10 to 20 minutes, depending on the size. Sliced frozen bread may be toasted without thawing.

Partially baked yeast breads

Yeast bread and rolls that are baked just long enough to destroy the action of the yeast and set the dough may be stored in your freezer for 3 months. Cool the partially baked breads, wrap them or package them in the same manner as the fully baked product, and freeze. Bake them, unthawed, in a moderate oven (350° F.) for about 30 minutes, or until they are golden brown. They will taste exactly like freshly baked bread.

Unbaked yeast breads

Unbaked bread and rolls are less satisfactory for freezing than the partially or fully baked product and should not be stored longer than 3 weeks. Make your favorite recipe, let the dough rise until it is double in bulk, and punch it down. Shape the dough into loaves, rolls, or coffee rings. Brush the surface with olive oil or melted sweet butter to prevent the dough from drying out and freeze. Remove them from the freezer as soon as they are frozen and package. Wrap loaves and coffee rings in moisture-vaporproof paper and seal. Package frozen rolls close together in shallow cartons with freezer paper between them.

The activity of the yeast is slowly destroyed in frozen unbaked yeast breads, so plan to use them in a short time. Even less storage time than a 3-week period results in fluffier, lighter breads.

To use, unwrap the frozen breads and let them rise, covered lightly, in a warm place away from drafts for 2 to 3 hours, or until light. Bake in the usual way.

Baking powder breads

Nut breads, fruit loaves, steamed brownbread, gingerbread, corn breads, baking powder biscuit, muffins, and other quick breads may be frozen before or after baking, but as in the case of yeast bread, they will hold for much longer periods if they are baked first. The unbaked products should not be stored for longer than 3 weeks. The baked will retain their freshness and flavor for as long as 6 months.

Nut and fruit breads and steamed brownbread should be thawed in their original wrappings at room temperature for 1 hour. Then, if you wish to serve them hot, place in a 350° F. oven for 15 to 20 minutes. Muffins, cornbread, and baking powder biscuits do not need to be thawed, but may be heated in a moderate oven directly from the freezer. Frozen waffles may be thawed and heated in a toaster.

SANDWICHES AND CANAPÉS

Sandwiches

Often it is advantageous to make sandwiches ahead of time for sandwich lunches, lunch boxes, teas, and evening snacks, and this can be accomplished with a home freezer.

Not all sandwich fillings freeze successfully. Lettuce, celery, cucumbers, fresh tomato slices, and other foods that should be crisp should not be used, for they lose their crispness on freezing. Jam and jelly filling are not good either, for the jelly soaks into the bread. Hard-cooked eggs are a poor choice, for the whites become tough and leathery.

Good sandwich fillings for frozen sandwiches are cheese and cheese spreads; sliced, cooked meats; poultry; sea food; and ham or liver spreads.

Cut bread very thinly and remove the crusts if you wish. Butter the bread to prevent a filling such as tuna-fish or crab-meat salad, deviled ham, or cream cheese from soaking into the bread. Wrap each sandwich separately and freeze. The sandwiches may be husky ones destined for the lunch box or dainty teatime ones in a variety of shapes—rolled, open face, ribbon, or checkerboard. Sandwiches packed in the lunch box directly from the freezer will be completely thawed and ready to be enjoyed by noon.

Sandwiches may be stored in the freezer for 1 month.

Canapés

Here again, not all canapés freeze well, but those that do are delicious and a great last-minute time saver. They can be made at your leisure weeks in advance of a party. Toasted canapés are particularly good in both texture and flavor. They remain much crisper than untoasted bread canapés and stay crisp for a couple of hours after they are thawed.

Butter thin slices of bread and cut them into strips, rounds, or triangles. Place the cut-outs on a buttered baking sheet and toast them in a moderate oven (350° F.) until they are golden. Place the filling on the toast and freeze the canapés on the baking sheet. As soon as they are frozen, pack an assortment in a carton, one or two dozen per carton, separating the layers with two sheets of freezer paper. Seal the cartons, label, and store in your freezer.

When you wish to serve canapés, remove them from the freezer 30 minutes before they will be needed. Place them on a serving tray, garnish them attractively, and let them thaw at room temperature.

Bread canapés such as tiny cheese rolls may be toasted in a moderate oven (350° F.) directly from the freezer and served hot.

Canapés may be stored in your freezer for 1 month.

CAKES

Cakes, baked and frosted or not as preferred, are frozen most satisfactorily. Angel food and butter cakes of all kinds freeze beautifully, although the texture of butter cakes may become finer and firmer during frozen storage. Fruitcakes actually improve with freezing. The flavors of the fruits and spices become blended; the cakes remain moist and do not crumble when sliced after they are thawed. Filled cakes are not recommended for freezing, as the filling is apt to soak into the cake and cause sogginess.

Baked cakes may be cut into family-sized portions before freezing.

Frosted cakes

Uncooked butter frostings made with confectioners' sugar are the best to use on cakes that are to be frozen. Boiled frostings crumble when cut after 2 to 3 weeks' storage and egg-white icings become frothy. Cool the cake thoroughly before icing or decorating. Place it on a sturdy cardboard base and put it in the freezer until the icing is solid. Remove and overwrap cardboard base and cake in moisture-vaporproof paper and return to the freezer.

Iced cakes must be unwrapped immediately after they are removed from the freezer to prevent the frosting from sticking to the wrappings. Let the cake thaw at room temperature for 30 to 40 minutes. Iced cakes should not be stored longer than 4 months.

Unfrosted cakes

Cool the cakes before wrapping them in moisture-vaporproof paper. Since cakes do not freeze solidly, some outer protection is needed to prevent them from being crushed during storage. Metal containers are best, but heavy cardboard cartons may be used. Wrap layers of cake separately and then wrap two or three together, depending on their ultimate use.

Fruitcakes do not need support. Wrap them in Cellophane, Plio-film, or Saran and overwrap with freezer paper or aluminum foil.

Cakes will thaw at room temperature in 30 to 40 minutes. Keep uniced cakes in their original wrappings to prevent moisture from condensing on the surface. Frozen cakes may be unwrapped and filled and frosted directly from the freezer.

Unfrosted angel food, sponge cakes, and butter cakes keep well for 6 to 8 months. Fruitcakes will keep a full year or longer.

Cake batters

While cake batters may be frozen, it is much better to freeze the baked cake. In an emergency, however, pour the batter into the utensil in which it is to be baked. Freeze the batter in the pan, then package pan and batter in moisture-vaporproof paper. Cup cakes may be frozen in paper baking cups in pans, removed from the pan when frozen, and packaged. Thaw batter for a large cake for about 1 hour at room temperature, then bake as usual. Batter frozen in 8-inch layer-cake pans may be baked without thawing at 375° F. for 35 to 40 minutes. Cupcakes need no thawing. Bake them directly from the freezer at 375° F. for 15 minutes. Reduce the oven temperature to 350° F. and continue to bake for 15 minutes longer. Do not store cake batters longer than 2 months.

COOKIES

Baked cookies or the cooky dough may be frozen, but there is little logic in occupying freezer space with the baked ones. Most baked cookies stay fresh in cooky jars for many days, longer at least than they can be preserved from a hungry household. I've never known cookies to go stale in my house. It's simply a question of finding enough time to keep a supply on hand. Freezing cooky dough is the answer. Making the dough takes very little time and most recipes can be doubled, tripled, or quadrupled without ill effects. It is cutting and baking the cookies that is the time-consuming part. So, make a large batch of dough, bake a jar full, and freeze

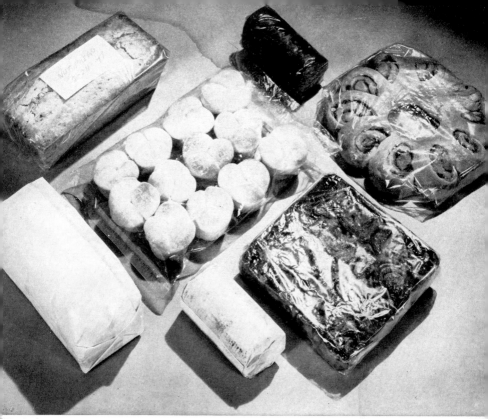

Westinghouse

Above: Many types of breads, rolls, and coffeecakes are easily frozen and may be packaged in a variety of ways. Double or triple your favorite recipes, your baking chores for a week or more are finished in a single afternoon, and your family will enjoy the flavor and goodness of home-baked products from your home freezer. **Below:** Baking powder or yeast rolls may be frozen before they are packaged, then placed close together in moisture-vaporproof cartons.

"Freezing Foods at Home"

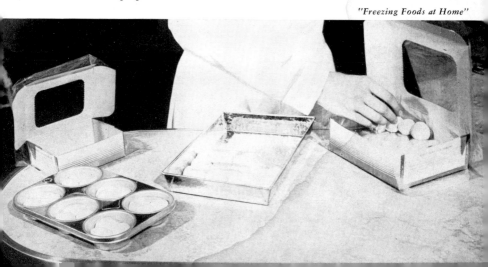

Above: Keep a supply of baked waffles in your freezer. To thaw, merely place a section in a pop-up toaster. When the waffle pops up it is done, hot, crisp, and delicious. **Below:** Frost a cake with uncooked butter frosting, place it on a sturdy cardboard base, and put it in the freezer until the icing is solid. Remove and overwrap cardboard base and cake in moisture-vaporproof paper and return to the freezer.

Westinghouse

Above: Baked cookies or the cooky dough may be frozen with excellent results. Freeze baked cookies in cartons, separating the layers with two sheets of freezer paper. Freeze drop cookies on a baking sheet and when frozen package them in cartons. They may be baked without thawing. **Below:** Freeze unbaked pies in pie plates. Lift them out of the plates, package, and return to the freezer. Only a minimum number of pie plates is necessary, using this method.

Frigidaire

This pleasant array of home-baked products is ready for storing in the "gift corner" of your home freezer. What could be nicer to have always available and ready for giving on special occasions? Shown above are tea rings, a novel cooky corsage, ready-baked rolls, nut bread loaves, plum pudding, white and dark fruitcakes, cookies, and a spring fruit pie made of pineapple, rhubarb, and strawberries.

the rest of the dough to cut or roll out and bake as needed. Many's the time when the oven is hot from a casserole, a cake, or a pie. While watching and waiting for the dish to come from the oven, the cookies can be cut and popped into the oven when the other food comes out. Time and temperature are both saved.

Baked cookies

Baked cookies will keep in your freezer for 8 months. Pack them in cartons, separating the layers with two sheets of freezer paper, overwrap, seal, label, and freeze. To use, simply thaw the cookies at room temperature.

Rolled cooky dough

Roll out the dough and cut it into various shapes. Stack the cut-out dough in cartons with 2 pieces of freezer paper between layers, overwrap, label, and freeze. They may be baked without thawing and will keep in your freezer for 6 months.

Unrolled cooky dough

Form the dough into long rolls or bricks, wrap, and freeze. Slice the dough while it is still frozen, place the slices on buttered baking sheets, and bake immediately. They will keep well for 6 months.

Drop cooky dough

Drop the dough on a baking sheet by the teaspoonful ¼ inch apart in exactly the same manner as if you were going to bake the cookies. Place them in the freezer until they are frozen. Remove the frozen drops of dough from the freezer and pack them by layers in cartons, with 2 sheets of freezer paper between layers. To bake, remove them from the carton without thawing, place them on a buttered baking sheet, and bake like the freshly made dough.

PIES

Pies, baked or unbaked, and pie shells, baked or unbaked, may be frozen for future use and, when you make a pie, it is almost as easy to make several. Bake and eat one. Freeze the rest. Then you will always have a pie ready to pop into the oven for either baking or heating. In general, pies that are frozen unbaked have flakier, more tender crusts and fresher flavor than those baked before freezing, and the very best are double-crust pies such as fruit, berry, or mince. But baked pie shells filled with chiffon mixtures and creams are also delicious. Meringue toppings toughen and separate during frozen storage, so save the topping to put on and brown in the oven before serving. Baked custard pies are not satisfactorily frozen, as the custard separates during storage.

Unbaked pies

Make pies in the usual way in metal, glass, or special metal-rimmed paper baking plates. They may be packaged and frozen in the pie plate or they may be frozen first, removed from the pie plate, and then wrapped. Package them in moisture-vaporproof wrappings and protect them from damage by inserting them in a carton. Unbaked frozen pies need no thawing. Bake them in a preheated oven (425° F.) for 15 to 20 minutes, reduce the heat to 375° F., and bake them for 30 minutes longer, or until the crust is golden. Don't store unbaked pies longer than 2 months.

Baked pies

Bake the pies and let them cool. Package them in the pie plate in moisture-vaporproof wrapping and freeze. Let them thaw for 30 to 45 minutes at room temperature, or thaw them in a slow oven (250 to 300° F.) for 30 minutes and serve them warm. Baked pies will keep for 6 months.

Filled pie shells

Baked pie shells filled with chiffon or cream mixtures should be frozen before they are wrapped. They must also be protected from damage by inserting the wrapped pie in a sturdy box or carton. Let them thaw at room temperature for 30 to 45 minutes. They may be garnished with whipped cream before they are frozen, or they may be topped with meringue after they are thawed and baked in the oven until the meringue is browned. They will keep well in your freezer for as long as 6 months.

CHAPTER NINE

Ready-cooked foods, leftovers, and frozen food menus

Once a busy housewife discovers that the real joy of a home freezer is in being able to store ready-cooked foods and entire meals and then merely heat and serve them, a home freezer becomes no longer a luxury or convenience, but an essential adjunct to modern living.

Ready-cooked meals in your freezer mean security. As an example, if you were confined to bed and could not perform the task of actually cooking a meal and presenting it to your family, you could, by remote control and your freezer, tell your husband or your child how to take a packaged meal from the freezer and cook it. In miraculous time a perfectly planned, well-balanced dinner can be on the table—a meal more than adequate to satisfy the requirements of your family.

Ready-cooked foods in your freezer add weeks, months, even years to your life in leisure hours, giving you time on your hands to enjoy your home and children, to join in your husband's "time off" at home, or to indulge at long last in those hobbies and outside interests for which you have never before had time.

Three meals every day are served in the average household. They can be moments of tiresome routine to be dispensed with as quickly as possible—necessary evils. Our bodies require vitamins, proteins, and carbohydrates, we know, and so we laboriously cook to replenish the losses of expended energy. But with a home freezer, most of the work and all of the drudgery can be finished in advance, when you have the time, energy, and enthusiasm to prepare meals. And it's just as easy to prepare and cook twice as much, even three times as much, of a dish, serve what you need, and freeze the rest for some future date.

Much of the food for special occasions, holiday meals, and dinner and luncheon parties may be prepared, cooked, and frozen weeks in advance, so that last-minute confusion and clutter in the kitchen are eliminated and you can present your relaxed, unruffled self to your guests—really glad to see them! For the first time in your life, *you* can actually enjoy your own parties. Course after course comes out of your freezer and into the stove to be reheated while you unconcernedly sip a cocktail in the living room with your guests.

As the doorbell rings, bring out a tray of cheese rolls and pop them into the oven. By the time drinks are served, the cheese rolls are ready to be served piping hot, golden brown. And so it goes— out of the freezer and into the oven, to be served with a minimum of effort and a maximum of flavor.

No longer is there such a thing as an "unexpected guest." You are ready and waiting for any number of guests to land in on you, whether for brunch, tea, cocktails, or dinner. You are smugly prepared for any emergency. Having to offer no excuses, you can present to your friends the warmth and hospitality of your home.

Unfortunately, this chapter can be only a beginning to the story of entire meals and the many ready-cooked dishes that can be stored in your freezer. Space in this book permits only a few facts, a few of my own favorite recipes, and suggestions to start you thinking along these time-saving lines. Consult other cookbooks for specific recipes not found here.

Don't be afraid to experiment. Practically every cooked food in the average housewife's repertoire can be frozen and you will certainly want to freeze your family's favorite dishes made from your pet recipes. You will discover that some freeze better than others. Maybe you will decide that the dish would be better had you left out a certain vegetable or spice, adding this particular ingredient to complete the recipe while the dish is being thawed and heated. Maybe it will be perfect as it is, providing you do not store it too long.

Some dishes keep their flavor and quality for many months; others for a few weeks only. So don't try to see how *long* you can store them. Leave the experiments in storage-life tests to recognized authorities in the freezing field. Store your ready-cooked foods for convenience and not for the dim future. As a general rule, don't plan to store them longer than 1 month for highest quality of flavor, texture, and eye appeal.

Right here it might be wise to remind you of the very few foods that have not yet been frozen and thawed satisfactorily. If you will stay away from these danger foods and remember the basic principles of packaging, you have little to worry about.

1. Cooked starch products such as potatoes, rice, and macaroni become soggy if frozen in a stew, soup, or sauce, though potato croquettes, Spanish rice, and macaroni and cheese all freeze well. It is only when the cooked starch product is immersed in a large quantity of liquid that it is unsatisfactory.

2. Salad vegetables that you wish to eat crisp cannot be frozen, as they lose their crispness.

3. Custards and some cream puddings or cake fillings are apt to curdle.

4. Gelatin salads and gelatin desserts do not hold up in frozen storage.

5. Mayonnaise will curdle.

6. Hard-cooked egg whites become tough and leathery.

SOUPS AND SOUP STOCKS

It's not hard to understand why the modern housewife does not have time to prepare all the ingredients that go into a good soup stock, or the inclination to stay home to keep a wary eye on the kettle as the stock chuckles over a gentle heat. A really good homemade stock requires lengthy simmering to bring it to perfection, and no longer do we do our cooking on an iron-topped stove where the *pot-au-feu* simmered quietly day in and day out as an integral part of every contented household.

But now, with the home freezer, a revival of the *pot-au-feu* is in fashion. Once a month, or once every two months, enough rich, fragrant stock can be made to satisfy the soup and sauce needs of your family. And once you put the soup kettle on the stove to distill the essence of meat, fowl, vegetables, and herbs, you will never again be without this important adjunct to domestic bliss.

There is nothing quite so stimulating a first course to a meal as hot consommé, served simply garnished with a little finely chopped parsley or dill, or with a tablespoon of cooked vegetables, noodles, or rice added to each serving, or topped with a spoonful of tiny squares of bread sautéed in butter until golden.

Almost any meat, fowl, or vegetable can be added to the soup kettle at whim. Here are basic recipes for beef and chicken broths.

Beef broth

1 pound veal knuckle
1½ pounds lean brisket
1 beef knuckle
4 chicken feet, cleaned and skinned
2 leeks
1 large onion stuck with 2 cloves
2 stalks celery with the leaves
4 sprigs parsley
6 peppercorns
3 quarts water
2 teaspoons salt

Put the veal knuckle, brisket, beef knuckle, chicken feet, vegetables, and peppercorns in a large soup kettle. Cover with the water and bring slowly to a boil. Remove the scum that rises to the surface and simmer the stock gently for 1 hour. Add the salt and continue to simmer for another hour, or until the meat is tender. Correct the seasoning and strain the broth through a fine sieve lined with cheesecloth. Cool, remove the fat, and package the broth in moisture-vaporproof, liquid-tight containers, leaving 1 inch headspace. Seal, label, and freeze.

Chicken broth

A 5-pound stewing hen
1 veal knuckle
4 chicken feet, cleaned and skinned
3 quarts water
2 teaspoons salt
6 peppercorns
3 leeks
2 carrots
1 onion stuck with 3 cloves
2 stalks celery
1 clove garlic
1 bay leaf
A pinch of thyme

Put the hen, veal knuckle, chicken feet, the water, salt, and peppercorns in a large soup kettle. Bring the water slowly to the boil and simmer for 1 hour, removing the scum as it accumulates on the surface. Add the remaining ingredients and continue to simmer for 1 hour longer. Correct the seasoning and strain the broth through a fine sieve lined with cheesecloth. Cool, remove the fat, and package the broth in moisture-vaporproof, liquid-tight containers, leaving 1 inch headspace. Seal, label, and freeze.

To thaw broths

Remove the broth from the package and heat it in a covered saucepan over a low flame for 45 minutes.

In warm weather the broth may be thawed overnight in the refrigerator and served as a refreshing jellied consommé, topped with finely chopped parsely mixed with minced onion and lemon juice.

Concentrated broths

Concentrated broths save freezer space. Make your stock, keeping it lightly seasoned with salt and pepper, and strain. Return the strained broth to the stove and simmer it gently until it is reduced to half, one third, or one quarter its original quantity. Package it in moisture-vaporproof, liquid-tight containers and be sure you label each container with the type of stock and the amount that it was concentrated. You will need to know that you must add 1 cup water for every cup of 50% concentrated stock, 2 cups water for every cup of 33⅓% concentrate, and 3 cups water for every 75% concentrate to make a consommé.

Concentrated stock may be frozen in ice-cube trays and packaged in little blocks in the same manner as is recommended for eggs (see Index). Many times you will want just that much concentrated stock to enrich a sauce or gravy, or to add to a chicken sauté.

Hearty soups

Many hearty soups make a nourishing meal in themselves, accompanied by hot French bread, baking powder biscuits, or corn bread. Make your favorite vegetable soup, your best minestrone, but leave out the macaroni, rice, or potatoes. These ingredients should be cooked later and added to the soup when it is reheated.

Keep on hand several containers of fish and sea-food chowders. Chowders that use milk or cream do not freeze too well. Leave out the milk or cream and add it when the soup is thawed. Remember to add this valuable bit of information to the label, or you may forget that an ingredient must be added to complete the chowder.

Navy-bean, black-bean, and lentil soups also freeze beautifully and they make more of those meal-in-one dishes that are a boon to any housewife. Add a tossed green salad to the menu, and serve a little cheese, or a bowl of fruit, for dessert.

Package soups in pint or quart containers, leaving ½ inch headspace in pints and 1 inch in quarts. Glass containers are good, but any container for soup must not only be moisture-vaporproof but liquid-tight as well. Seal, label intelligently, and freeze.

Thaw heavy soups in a covered saucepan over a gentle flame for 1 hour.

READY-COOKED VEGETABLES

As you already know, if you read the vegetable chapter, not many ready-cooked vegetables freeze well, but fortunately the ones that do freeze well are those long-cooking vegetables such as yams, pumpkins, squash, whole beets, and beans, which take time and fuel to prepare for a meal. Vegetable purées also freeze well, and for these you should refer to the vegetable chapter or the index.

The average vegetable, whether fresh or frozen, takes only a matter of minutes to ready it for the table and presents little problem to the busy housewife. So when you do have time, prepare a large quantity of the longer-cooking, time-consuming vegetables that you want to store in your freezer to add variety and color to your daily meals. Most of these take 30 minutes to thaw and reheat in a moderate oven, so to save fuel, plan to serve them when the oven is already busy cooking a roast or heating a casserole.

Potatoes

Cooked potatoes, both white and sweet, can be successfully stored in your freezer. Keep on hand a few packages of French fries and candied sweet potatoes (see Chapter V) for quick meals.

Freshly mashed potatoes, whipped until light with milk or cream and butter, may be frozen in pint or quart containers ready to thaw and heat over boiling water, or they may be formed into potato croquettes or patties and packaged in layers with two sheets of freezer paper between layers for easy separation before they are thawed. They need no thawing before heating, but may be browned slowly on both sides in butter in a skillet or in the oven, directly from the frozen state. Sweet potatoes may be treated in the same way.

Baked white or sweet potatoes may also be frozen. Bake yams or sweet potatoes, halve them, and cool. Re-form each potato with two layers of freezer paper between the halves and wrap each re-formed potato individually. White potatoes may be baked and stuffed. Cut the baked potatoes in half and scoop out the pulp. Mash the pulp with cream, butter, and seasonings and refill the halves, piling the potato purée high in the center. Freeze and when frozen wrap each filled potato half in moisture-vaporproof freezer paper and store in freezer.

Thaw baked white or sweet potatoes in a moderate oven (325° F.) for 30 minutes.

Potato chips or French fried potatoes should not be stored for longer than 6 weeks. Other cooked potatoes may be kept from 4 to 6 months.

SWEET POTATOES CECILIA

Here is a sweet-potato casserole that freezes well and makes an excellent buffet dish. It may be frozen in the casserole. When needed, remove the casserole from the freezer and put it in a cold oven. Heat the oven to 325° F. and bake the casserole for 1 hour. If the sweet potatoes are frozen in a Pyrex baking dish, the dish may be taken from the freezer and put into a preheated oven with no danger of the casserole breaking. Before baking, dot the surface with butter and sprinkle with cinnamon.

>   *3 pounds sweet potatoes*
>   *½ cup butter*
>   *½ cup sherry*
>   *¼ teaspoon nutmeg*
>   *¼ teaspoon cinnamon*
>   *Milk*
>   *Salt and pepper to taste*

Boil the potatoes in their jackets until soft, peel, and put through a ricer. Add the butter, sherry, nutmeg, and cinnamon and beat the mixture until the potatoes are light. Add a little milk if the potatoes are dry and season the purée with salt and pepper to taste. Cool thoroughly and turn the purée into a buttered baking dish. Wrap the dish in moisture-vaporproof paper and freeze. Do not store longer than 1 month.

Squash and pumpkin

All varieties of winter squash and pumpkin can be cooked, puréed, and frozen for use as a vegetable, in pies, or in puddings (see Chapter V). Baked acorn squash is a nice "variety" vegetable to store in your freezer and will keep well for 4 to 6 months. Bake the halved squash according to your favorite recipe, until barely tender. Cool, package each half individually in moisture-vaporproof paper, and freeze. Thaw in a moderate oven (325° F.) in a baking dish containing 1 inch of hot water for 30 minutes.

Peppers

In the fall, when peppers are at their peak, in the stores or on the vine, they may be stuffed with rice, cottage cheese, shrimp, combinations of rice and sea food, or almost any leftover and stored in your freezer for as long as 4 months to make economical and appetizing luncheon dishes. One of my favorite stuffings is made with ground round steak and is sufficient for 10 peppers.

STUFFED PEPPERS

> *2 onions, chopped*
> *1 pound round steak, ground*
> *4 fresh tomatoes, peeled and chopped*
> *4 tablespoons butter*
> *Salt and pepper to taste*
> *2 cups fresh bread crumbs*
> *10 peppers*
> *⅔ cup fine dry buttered bread crumbs*

Sauté the onions, ground steak, and tomatoes in the butter until the onion is soft and transparent. Season the mixture with salt and pepper to taste and mix with the soft fresh bread crumbs.

Remove the stems, seeds, and membranes from 10 large green peppers and parboil the peppers for 3 minutes in boiling salted water. Drain the peppers and fill them with the stuffing. Sprinkle the stuffing with fine dry bread crumbs and freeze the peppers. When frozen, wrap each pepper in moisture-vaporproof paper and package 4 or 5, as desired, in one package. Overwrap and store.

To thaw: Unwrap the stuffed peppers directly from the freezer and put them in a buttered baking dish. Top each pepper with ½ teaspoon butter and bake the peppers in a moderate oven (350° F.) for about 30 minutes.

Beans, baked

What is the most popular accompaniment to any buffet supper, whether it be a simple late after-the-theater, intimate meal, or an elaborate dinner-buffet? You guessed it—baked beans. And baked beans will keep well in your freezer for as long as 1 year. Bake the beans New England style, or according to your favorite recipe, or try my favorite, seasoned with garlic and sage.

BAKED BEANS WATCH HILL FARM

2 pounds white beans
1 pound salt pork
2 onions
3 cloves of garlic
½ teaspoon powdered sage
Salt to taste
½ teaspoon pepper
2 teaspoons dry mustard
½ teaspoon allspice

Wash the beans and soak them overnight. Drain, cover them generously with fresh cold water, and add the salt pork, onions, garlic, sage, salt, and pepper. Bring the water slowly to a boil, cover the kettle, and simmer the beans for 1½ to 2 hours, or until the skins burst easily, adding more boiling water if necessary from time to time.

Remove and slice the salt pork. Line the bottom of a large casserole or bean pot with slices of the meat and fill the pot with beans. Bury the onions in the center of the beans and arrange the remaining meat slices on top. Dissolve the mustard in 1 cup of the bean water and pour it over the beans. Sprinkle with the allspice, cover the casserole, and bake in a moderate oven (325° F.) for 3 to 4 hours, adding more of the bean water as needed. Uncover the casserole for the last hour.

Cool the beans and package them in pint or quart cartons or bags. The containers must be moisture-vaporproof. Seal and freeze.

To cook: Remove the beans from the container and put them in a baking dish. Cover the dish and bake the beans in a moderate oven (325° F.) for 1½ hours.

READY-COOKED MEATS

Almost any kind of cooked meats may be frozen satisfactorily. The only ones to avoid are fried steaks and chops which, while edible after a month in frozen storage, have lost some of their original flavor and crispness.

The storage time for various kinds of cooked meats varies from 2 weeks to 6 months. Chile con carne, for example, will retain its original flavor and texture for as long as 6 months. Hashes made from corned beef or other cooked meats and baked ham may be stored for 4 months, while sliced cooked meats, packaged plain or covered with gravy, meat loaves, and meat balls, sauced or plain, should be used within 2 weeks, or 4 at the very longest.

Many meat dishes, such as broiled chops, sautéed lamb kidneys, veal *scaloppine, shish kebab,* and so on take only moments to prepare and little would be gained by cooking and freezing them. It would actually take longer to thaw and reheat them than to cook them when needed. It is wiser by far to concentrate on those meat dishes that require long cooking.

Fortunately braised meats, pot roasts, and stews that require many hours of slow cooking over gentle heat will keep in frozen storage for 6 months. The time to ready them for the table is so much less than the actual cooking time that you will save many hours of keeping a wary eye on the kettle, as well as a substantial amount of electricity or gas.

Many of these dishes make attractive casseroles for entertaining and buffet suppers, so it is most practical and time-saving to make a large quantity of any of these long-cooked braised meats and freeze for future use the portion not eaten for dinner that night.

Remember to omit potatoes, rice, noodles, spaghetti, or macaroni from meat stews to be frozen. Any of these ingredients can be cooked and added to the dish while the frozen product is being heated. No time is lost and the starchy foods will be fresh and not sodden with juice.

In addition to the meat dishes which require long cooking, you will undoubtedly want to prepare in advance many of your favorite meat dishes to have on hand for quick emergency meals. Some excellent remainders that freeze well are veal birds, Swedish meat balls, and curry of lamb.

All meat dishes must be cooled and thoroughly chilled before they are packaged and frozen.

Stew may be frozen right in the casserole in which it was made. Once solidly frozen it may be removed from the casserole to save freezer space, wrapped, and stored. To cook the stew, return it in its frozen state to its original container.

Or stew, chili con carne, chop suey, and so on may be packed in either pint or quart containers that are moisture-vaporproof and liquid-tight. Use the size best suited to your family's needs.

Baked ham and meat loaves should be carefully wrapped in Saran, Pliofilm, or Cellophane and overwrapped with stockinette, but if a laminated freezer paper is used, no overwrap is necessary.

To serve stew, remove as many packages as needed and turn the stew into a casserole, or baking dish. Heat the stew in a moderate oven (325° F.) for 1 hour, or turn it into a saucepan, cover, and heat over a low flame for 1 hour.

Baked ham requires 15 minutes per pound in a 350° F. oven to thaw and reheat. Meat loaves may be thawed, sliced, and served cold, or they may be put directly into a 350° F. oven and reheated for 1 hour.

And now for a few of my favorite braised dishes that need only a dish of noodles, rice, or potatoes to make a perfect meal. Add a tossed green salad and a simple dessert of frozen fruit, thawed but still frosty, and what could be more delectable for family or friends?

Boeuf bourguignonne

6 pounds chuck steak, cubed
Flour
¼ pound butter
½ cup olive oil
Salt and pepper
½ cup warm cognac
½ pound bacon, diced
4 cloves garlic, chopped
2 carrots, chopped
2 leeks, chopped
2 tablespoons chopped parsley
4 onions, chopped
2 bay leaves
½ teaspoon dry thyme
1 bottle red wine
1 tablespoon flour
2 tablespoons butter
3 tablespoons Kitchen Bouquet

Roll the chuck steak in flour and brown it over a high flame in the butter and olive oil. Sprinkle the meat with salt and pepper, pour the cognac over it, and blaze. Transfer the meat and juices to a larger casserole.

Sauté the bacon until it is crisp. Add the garlic, carrots, leeks, parsley, and onions and continue to sauté until the vegetables are lightly browned. Transfer to the casserole.

Add to the casserole the bay leaves, thyme, and red wine and add enough water to cover the meat and vegetables. Cook the casserole, covered, in a moderate oven (350° F.) for 1½ to 2 hours.

Work 1 tablespoon flour and 2 tablespoons butter to a smooth paste and stir it into the sauce in the casserole with the Kitchen Bouquet. Cover and continue to cook for 2 to 3 hours longer. The longer this dish cooks, the better it will be. Remove the casserole from the oven to cool.

Heat 2 pounds small onions in 2 tablespoons butter. Sprinkle them with 1 teaspoon sugar and cook, stirring, until the onions are browned. Add ¼ cup red wine, cover, and cook gently for 20 minutes.

Sauté 1 pound mushroom caps in 2 tablespoons butter and 2 tablespoons olive oil until they are golden brown. Sprinkle them with the juice of ½ lemon and turn to brown the other side.

Add the onions to the casserole and arrange the mushrooms on top. Cover the casserole and chill the stew in the refrigerator overnight. Remove the cover from the casserole, wrap the casserole in moisture-vaporproof paper, and freeze.

Or the stew may be packaged in 4 quart containers, and the onions and mushrooms packaged separately.

To thaw, empty the stew into a casserole, top with the onions and mushrooms, and cover tightly. Heat the casserole in a moderate oven (350° F.) for 1½ hours. Serve sprinkled with finely chopped parsley. Whipped potatoes may be served with the stew, or boiled potatoes may be added to the casserole before it is served.

Hungarian goulash

1 cup bacon drippings
3 pounds top round steak cut into 1½-inch squares
2 pounds onions, peeled and sliced
1 bottle of ale
1 cup tomato paste
1 bay leaf
Salt and pepper
2 teaspoons paprika

Heat the bacon drippings in a large heavy kettle and add the meat. Sear over a high flame until the meat is well browned on all sides. Add the onions, lower the flame, and continue to cook for 10 minutes. Add the ale, tomato paste, and bay leaf. Cover the kettle tightly and cook over a very low heat for about 2½ hours, or until the meat is tender. Season the goulash with salt and pepper and stir in the paprika, being careful to keep the paprika from burning onto the sides of the pot.

Cool, chill, package, and freeze. Makes about 1 quart and 1 pint of goulash, which would serve 6 well. The recipe may be doubled or tripled.

Serve with wide egg noodles cooked until tender in a large quantity of boiling salted water and drained. Brown ½ cup bread crumbs in melted butter with 1 clove of garlic, chopped, and toss with the hot noodles.

Osso buco

> *3 pounds shank bones of veal cut into serving pieces 3*
> *inches long*
> *Flour*
> *½ cup olive oil*
> *Salt and pepper*
> *2 cups meat stock*
> *1 cup white wine*
> *1 clove garlic*
> *½ teaspoon basil*
> *4 tomatoes, peeled, seeded, and chopped*
> *2 onions, peeled and finely chopped*
> *3 sprigs of parsley*

Dredge the pieces of veal shanks in flour and sear them in the hot olive oil until well browned. Sprinkle them with salt and pepper and add the meat stock and white wine. There should be enough liquid to half-cover the shanks. Bring the liquid to a boil, cover, and simmer for 20 minutes. Add the garlic, basil, tomatoes, onions, and parsley, cover, and continue to simmer for about 2 hours, or until the meat is tender.

Remove the meat to a platter to cool and boil the sauce until it is reduced and slightly thickened. Correct the seasoning and cool the sauce. Package meat and sauce in quart containers and freeze.

Serve the *osso buco* with quick-cooking rice, baked in the oven in veal or chicken broth while the stew is thawing and heating.

Ox-tail ragout

2 ox-tails, cut into serving pieces
2 pounds shin of beef with bone
1 large onion stuck with 2 cloves
1 bay leaf
3 quarts water
2 carrots
2 stalks celery
Salt and pepper

Put all the ingredients in a soup kettle, bring to a boil, removing the scum as it accumulates on the surface, and simmer for 3 hours, or until the meat is tender. Cool the meat in the broth. Discard the fat from the surface of the broth and remove the meat. Reheat the broth and strain through a sieve lined with cheesecloth.

4 tablespoons butter
1 clove garlic, minced
6 carrots, halved or quartered
10 small onions, peeled
½ cup diced celery
2 tablespoons flour
3 cups oxtail broth (freeze the rest for future use)
½ cup red wine

Melt the butter in a saucepan and brown the vegetables in it. Sprinkle the vegetables with the flour and mix well. Add the broth and red wine and bring the liquid to a boil. Add the ox-tails and simmer for 30 minutes, or until the vegetables are tender.

Cool the ragout, chill in the refrigerator, and package. Makes 1 quart and 1 pint container and serves 6.

To serve, turn the frozen ragout into a casserole and heat it in a moderate oven (325° F.) for 1 hour. Sprinkle with 2 tablespoons finely chopped parsley and serve with boiled potatoes.

COOKED FISH AND SEA FOOD

Creamed fish, lobster and shrimp Newburg, lobster Thermidor, cooked lobster tails, and shrimp may all be prepared and stored in your freezer for 2 to 4 weeks. But since most fish dishes can be quickly prepared from either the fresh or frozen raw fish, little seems to be gained by freezing the prepared dish.

There may be a time when a cooked fish dish such as *coquille Saint-Jacques* or a deviled crab seems to be just right to complete an otherwise perfect menu and if you wish to prepare it in advance, your home freezer is at your service.

Fish or sea food baked in individual shells or ramekins and stored in your freezer can add variety to many a menu. They may be served as a first course to a dinner, or as a luncheon dish.

Baked sea food in shells

1 cup shrimp, cut into small pieces
1 cup crab meat
1 cup bay scallops
4 tablespoons butter
Salt and pepper
3 cups cream sauce
Buttered crumbs
Grated Parmesan cheese

Combine the shrimp, crab meat, and scallops and sauté them in the butter for 4 or 5 minutes, stirring constantly. Sprinkle the fish with salt and pepper to taste and stir in the cream sauce. Divide the mixture among 8 individual shells or ramekins and sprinkle generously with butter crumbs and cheese.

Freeze the sea food, then wrap each shell or ramekin individually in moisture-vaporproof paper and return to your freezer.

To serve, unwrap the shells and bake them in a moderate oven (350° F.) for 30 minutes.

POULTRY

Turkeys, geese, chickens, ducks, and poultry of all kinds may be cooked completely, plain or stuffed, and stored in your freezer ready for warming up in a moderate oven. Your Christmas or New Year's turkey may be stuffed with your favorite dressing and roasted to golden perfection as long as a month before the holiday.

Stuffed roast poultry

Stuff, truss, and roast the bird. As soon as it is cooked, discard the trussings, carefully remove all the stuffing, and put it in a casserole or baking dish. This *must* be done in order to prevent the possible spoilage of the dressing deep in the center of the bird, where it would take hours to cool were it not removed. Cool the bird and the stuffing partially, then put them in the refrigerator for 2 to 3 hours to chill thoroughly.

Pour off half the drippings from the roasting pan into a small, moisture-proof, liquid-tight container to freeze as soon as it is cool, for later use in basting the bird when it is reheated. Use the rest of the drippings in the pan to make a pan gravy. Cool the gravy, package, label, and freeze.

Wrap the bird tightly and carefully in moisture-vaporproof paper and freeze. Wrap the dressing, baking dish and all, in similar paper, label, and freeze.

To reheat the bird and stuffing: Allow 5 hours per pound thawing time, in the refrigerator, to thaw the bird completely. In the case of a turkey, it may be necessary to remove it from the freezer a good two days before you want to serve it. Return the thawed cooked bird to the roasting pan, add the drippings, and brush the bird generously with softened butter. Cook it in a moderate oven (325° F.) for 1 hour, basting frequently with the drippings.

The stuffing needs no preliminary thawing. Remove it from the freezer, cover the baking dish, and put it in the oven with the bird to thaw and heat.

Chicken or turkey pies, family size or individual, cooked and then frozen, are a convenient dish to have on hand for emergency meals. They may be stored for as long as 6 months and in just about 1 hour can be served hot and succulent directly from your freezer. The topping of the pie may be made of pie dough, baking powder biscuit dough, or fluffy mashed potatoes. The pies may be frozen in a glass baking dish or in crockery casseroles and reheated in the same casseroles without any preliminary thawing.

Chicken or turkey pies

Pie dough
1½ pounds sliced cooked chicken, or turkey
12 small boiled new potatoes
6 carrots, quartered and cooked
1 cup cooked peas
12 small cooked onions
12 mushroom caps, sautéed in butter
4 tablespoons butter or chicken fat
4 tablespoons flour
2 cups hot chicken stock
Salt and pepper to taste

Line a shallow baking dish with pie dough and in it arrange the chicken and vegetables.

In a saucepan melt the butter or chicken fat and stir in the flour. Gradually stir in the chicken stock and cook, stirring, until the sauce is smooth and thickened. Season with salt and pepper to taste. Pour the sauce over the chicken and vegetables in the baking dish. Cover the mixture with pie dough, press the edges of the dough firmly together, and cut slits in the top for the escape of steam. Bake the pie in a hot oven (425° F.) for 25 minutes, or until the crust is nicely browned.

Cool the pie and chill it thoroughly. Wrap it in moisture-vapor-proof paper, label, and freeze.

To thaw: Remove the pie from the freezer and place it directly in a moderate oven (325° F.) for 1 hour.

Creamed chicken or turkey is another appetizing dish which can be ready to serve in an hour or less and which retains its quality in frozen storage for 6 to 8 months. When mushrooms and green pepper or pimiento are added, creamed chicken becomes

Chicken à la king for 6

1 cup sliced mushrooms
3 tablespoons butter or chicken fat
3 tablespoons flour
1 cup hot chicken stock
1 cup cream
2 cups diced, cooked chicken
3 tablespoons chopped pimiento
Salt and pepper to taste

Sauté the mushrooms in the butter or chicken fat for 3 minutes. Stir in the flour and add gradually the chicken stock, stirring constantly. Continue to cook, stirring, until the sauce is smooth and thick. Stir in the cream and add the chicken, mushrooms, and pimiento. Add salt and pepper to taste and flavor the sauce, if desired, with sherry or Madeira.

Cool the chicken *à la* king and chill it thoroughly in the refrigerator. Package it in moisture-vaporproof, liquid-tight containers, seal, label, and freeze.

To serve: Turn the chicken *à la* king from the container into a saucepan and cook it, covered, for 1 hour over simmering water, stirring occasionally. Serve in patty shells; on toast, hot biscuits, squares of corn bread, or English muffins; in a noodle ring; rolled in thin pancakes, or with hot rice.

OTHER COOKED FOODS

Gravies, sauces for barbecues, and sauces for spaghetti may all be prepared according to your favorite recipe, cooled, and frozen for 1 to 2 months. Spaghetti, rice, and macaroni may be cooked, rinsed in cold water, drained well, and stored for 6 months in your freezer. If these starch foods are combined with vegetables or sauce, they should not be stored for longer than 2 to 4 weeks.

LEFTOVERS

With a home freezer, the stigma can be forever erased from the word *leftover*. As much as you may relish a turkey, a ham, or a roast of beef, no one wants to eat the leftovers from a roast several more times that same week. Your freezer is the perfect solution to mealtime monotony, for leftovers of all kinds may be frugally frozen and served as long as 2 weeks later, when they seem to be an entirely new meal and not a pallid reminder of yesterday's dinner.

Slice leftover roasts and wrap the slices compactly in moisture-vaporproof paper, or, if you have time, make the meat or poultry into ready-to-serve dishes, creamed dishes, casseroles, croquettes, et cetera. The details for wrapping and freezing and the maximum storage times for these prepared dishes have already been given in this chapter.

Plastic refrigerator dishes are ideal for storing leftover soups, stews, and gravies. They can be washed and used over and over again. With tight-fitting lids, they may be simply filled and the lid fitted down securely in place. Without lids, smooth aluminum foil down firmly over the top of the dish. Or wrap the entire dish in Saran wrap. Even the Saran wrap may be used again.

FROZEN FOOD MENUS

Entire meals—for emergencies, for everyday use, for special holiday dinners, or for parties—may be prepared in advance and stored in your home freezer. Whether you prepare and freeze every dish for the menu or whether you buy commercially frozen products to store in your freezer, you may like the idea of packaging every item for one meal together in a large bag and labeling the contents. Perhaps you will want to include on the label the menu and simple heating directions, or you might like simply to number the bag and keep on hand a little log book which lists not only the menu by number and the steps for preparing it, but any foods that you should have on hand to complete the meal, such as butter, cream, milk, salad greens, condiments, and coffee.

No matter how many menus were printed in this book, they could be but a beginning to a long story, and no amount of menus could hope to appeal to the particular likes and dislikes of every household. The menus that follow are meant to be only suggestions that I hope will provide sufficient inspiration to help you in planning your own meals and show you one way of deriving the very best value from your home freezer.

A week of family dinners from your freezer

*The starred items cannot be frozen.

SUNDAY

>Fruit Cup
>Roast Pork
>Candied Sweet Potatoes
>Buttered String Beans
>Applesauce
>Brown-and-serve Rolls
>Ice Cream Roll

MONDAY

>Minestrone
>Spaghetti with Tomato Sauce
>Tossed Green Salad*
>Garlic French Bread
>Angel Food Cake

TUESDAY

> Hungarian Goulash
> Buttered Noodles
> Hot Rolls
> Salad*
> Ice Cream with Fruit Sauce

WEDNESDAY

> Individual Chicken Pies with Whipped Potato Topping
> Endive Salad*
> Strawberry Tarts

THURSDAY

> Vegetable Soup
> Broiled Lamb Chops
> French Fried Potatoes
> Buttered Peas
> Apple Pie with Cheese

FRIDAY

> Tomato Juice
> Fish Filets Sautéed with Lemon Butter
> Baby Lima Beans
> Hot Rolls
> Cucumber in Sour Cream*
> Chocolate Cake

SATURDAY

> Broiled Steak with Mushrooms
> Baked Stuffed Potatoes
> Buttered Broccoli
> Fruit Salad
> Cream Puffs

A week of family suppers from your freezer

*The starred items cannot be frozen.

SUNDAY

> Vegetable Soup
> Salad*
> Hot French Bread
> Chocolate Eclairs

MONDAY

> Frankfurters and Baked Beans
> Pumpernickel Bread
> Ice Cream
> Cookies

TUESDAY

> Beef Stew
> Salad*
> Hot Rolls
> Butterscotch Pudding

WEDNESDAY

> Tomato Juice
> Chicken *à la* king
> Corn Muffins
> Applesauce
> Cake

THURSDAY

> Sautéed Sausages
> Sweet Potato Casserole
> Baking Powder Biscuits
> Blueberry Pie

FRIDAY

>Spaghetti with Meat Sauce
>Salad*
>Garlic Bread
>Lemon Ice

SATURDAY

>Hamburgers with Barbecue Sauce
>Potato Croquettes
>Salad*
>Baked Apple

One delightful way of casual entertaining is the casserole buffet. You may make your own favorite casserole such as chicken Marengo, chicken *cacciatore,* or one of the few meat stew recipes given in this book a week or two in advance and store casserole and all, well wrapped of course, in your freezer until the evening of your party. All you need to complement any of these meal-in-one dishes is a large tossed green salad, hot French bread, and a bottle or two of a good wine.

The salad greens can be washed, dried, and kept crisp and fresh in the refrigerator in a plastic bag, or wrapped in Saran paper, all ready to be tossed with lemon juice and a good French olive oil. An hour before your guests arrive, take the casserole from the freezer and put it in a moderate oven to thaw and heat. All you have to do is enjoy your guests until they are ready to enjoy your supper.

You may wish to complete the meal with an elaborate Baked Alaska put into a hot oven for 5 minutes directly from your freezer, or a large bowl of raspberry sherbet topped with thawed, but still frosty, halved peaches, or pineapple slices thawed in rum or kirsch and freshly baked cookies. But no matter how fancy or simple your dessert, your evening will be a sure-fire success and you will never have had such fun at your own party with your home freezer as

a silent, trusted servant and a minimum of pots and pans to wash
before you go happily to bed!

For those who like more formal entertaining, the home freezer
can serve up a more elaborate dinner as easily as a family one.

Holiday and company dinners from your freezer

*The starred items cannot be frozen.

Hot Consommé
Broiled Chicken with Tarragon Butter
Lima Beans in Cream
Saffron Rice
Hot Rolls
Salad*
Peaches Thawed in Cognac
Petits Fours

Fruit Cup
Roast Turkey with Chestnut Dressing
Giblet Gravy
Cranberry-Orange Relish
Sweet Potato Puffs
Green Beans with Tiny Onions and Mushrooms
Hot Rolls
Plum Pudding with Hard Sauce

Mushroom Soup
Roast Wild Duck Bigarade
Wild Rice
Buttered Peas
Hot French Bread
Salad*
Meringue Shells with Ice Cream

Crab Meat Cocktail
Veal Birds in White Wine
Broccoli
Baked Acorn Squash
Avocado Salad*
Cherries Jubilee

Turtle Soup
Broiled Shrimp
Roast Pheasants
Grilled Mushrooms
Potato Croquettes
Endive and Beet Salad*
Ice Cream Pie

For those with limited freezer space, or little time to prepare their own dishes for "meals from your freezer," here are a few menu suggestions that can be compiled from the wide variety of commercially frozen foods available today. Package each complete meal in a large bag, remove it when needed, and within 30 minutes you and your family can sit down to a hot, delicious dinner.

Quick menu suggestions compiled from commercially frozen products

*The starred items cannot be frozen.

MENU NO. 1

Onion Soup
Broiled Mixed Grill (Lamb Chops, Tiny Sausages, and
    Bacon)
Succotash
Hot Rolls
Ice Cream with Strawberry Topping

MENU NO. 2

Hot Consommé
Broiled Steak
Green Beans
French Fried Potatoes
Hot French Bread
Salad*
Cheese Cake

MENU NO. 3

Tomato Juice
Broiled Swordfish Steak
Green Peas
Cauliflower
Brown-and-serve Rolls
Fruit Cup
Cookies

MENU NO. 4

Shrimp Cocktail
Southern Fried Chicken
Whole Kernel Corn
Whipped Potatoes
Brown-and-serve French Bread
Asparagus *vinaigrette*
Apple Pie
Ice Cream

MENU NO. 5

Vegetable Soup
Broiled Ham Steak
Puréed Squash
Spinach
Parkerhouse Rolls
Fruit Salad
Ribbon Cake

MENU NO. 6

Melon Balls
Broiled African Lobster Tails
Broccoli
French Fried Potatoes
Tossed Salad*
Peach Shortcake

Index

Index

RECOMMENDED
FOR PREPARED FOODS

Product	Months
Yeast bread and rolls, baked	6
Yeast bread and rolls, partially baked	3
Yeast bread and rolls, unbaked	⅔
Baking powder breads, baked	6
Baking powder breads, unbaked	⅔
Cakes, baked unfrosted	6-8
Cakes, baked frosted	4
Fruitcakes, baked	12
Cake batters	2
Pies, baked	6
Pies, unbaked	2
Pie shells, filled	6
Cookies, baked	8
Cooky dough	6
Sandwiches and canapés	1
Soups	2
Macaroni and rice, plain	6
Macaroni and rice casserole dishes	½-1
Squash, acorn	4-6
Yams and sweet potatoes	1